LEAVINGS

Memoir of a 1920s Hollywood Love Child

Megan McClard

Aristata Press

Library of Congress Control Number: 2022916299

Project Coordinators: Judy Blankenship and Anne McClard

Book Design: Anne McClard and Michael McClard

Cover Design: Anne McClard

Editors: Jenefer Angell, Judy Blankenship and Elizabeth McClard

ISBN 978-1-7362316-2-3 (heirloom edition)

ISBN 978-1-7362316-0-9 (paper)

ISBN 978-1-7362316-3-0 (hardcover)

ISBN 978-1-7362316-1-6 (ebook)

Aristata Press, Portland, Oregon

For my children and their children and their children.

Life can only be understood backwards,

but it must be lived forwards.

Søren Kierkegaard

Contents

INTRODUCTION

Even before I went to college the first time, way back in 1946 (while all the characters were still alive), I wanted to write about my family. What I knew about them only filled a few pages and I ran out of words before I ran out of the green ink in my fountain pen. Twenty-five years later, finishing up eight years at University of Denver trying to master the craft of writing, I decided the project was so complex that I needed to write a trilogy.

In 1969, I devised a plan: I would begin with Juneau's story. I would base my dissertation project on her. I had typed and retyped fewer than a hundred pages before I realized that I really didn't have any idea who my oldest sister was or what she was doing there on that beach where she was murdered.

Years later, still trying to work it out, I was greatly saddened in the late summer of 1979 to learn that my longtime friend, Marta Mustain, was dying of cancer. Or, rather, living with it—still a wild woman, as she had always been. My sister Mardie's closest friend from the mid-1930s, I somehow inherited a portion of their friendship, as a kind of trust fund. Marta became one of my two biggest boosters. When I decided to go back to school, she thought it was a great idea. Instead of joining the chorus

Photo of me, at age 93, 2021, taken by Judy Blankenship

telling me that my greatest responsibility was to my five children, she went right out and found a great babysitter. She said that any time a woman aspired to do something that seemed out of her reach, the whole world said, "Down, girl!" Beyond that, she knew the McKenzies, my mother's family, inside out. She knew their secrets, their reputation, and their pride. She had even met my father. She liked him. (That was important to me, because I had heard so many negative things and I was, after all, his flesh and blood. How often had I heard "Just like Chaunce" when I did something or used some expression?)

The last time I saw Marta, we hugged and said our goodbyes; then she added, "Tell it like it is."

I said that I would try. And I have tried—so many times. I gave up on fiction a long time ago. One can't "tell it like it is" when one is fictionalizing in order to "protect the innocent." So a few years ago, I decided to write a history of my pretty much inconsequential life. On the one hand, it seemed an arrogant thing to do, self-centered; but still, I so wanted to tell my kids about the world I lived in, the people I knew and loved. On the other hand, it at some point occurred to me that the reason humans live so long after their breeding and nurturing days are over is to pass on their knowledge, to tell the members of their tribe where the water is, which plants are edible, which ones can make one happier than there is any obvious reason to be, and which ones bring on convulsions and/or hallucinations.

Yes, we elders must have been quite important back in the old days. Before there were written languages or paper or ink, old people were books. Some very old men mistook themselves for libraries.

Now, in the dawn of the twenty-first century, we have the internet and GPS. Books are old hat. Books are troublesome. They get dusty, dated, and have to be re-shelved. They can harbor disease. Even great university libraries are digitizing themselves and moving the books that are light enough to budge to depositories. Serious scholars demand space-saving electronic devices to filter, organize, reduce, and store bulky, stuffy stuff to naughts and ones. Not that it is a bad thing! I wouldn't have been able to put together much of any of the pieces of the jigsaw of my mother's, my father's, or my sister's lives without the internet. Much of what I have found came almost like magic. For example, when I went to look up "iron lung," so that my kids could see what it was like, of all of the bizarre coincidences a picture of my foster sister, DeLoris, popped up first thing. The internet is magnificent.

Certainly no one on earth needs to put up with the babbling of a toothless granny to find out the secrets of where to find water now that anyone can buy it in bottles on any corner. So, I wondered what I was supposed to be doing. Then it hit me. I had always had a lot of questions, things that I just wanted to know. Some things that I wanted to know just for the hell of it and some I felt I needed to know. I mean, what is the point, exactly, of being born? And the questions I never pondered when they were here: Who were those strangers that had created me? Why were they so weird, so out of touch? Why was it that we never understood each other? Wouldn't it have been great if they had explained themselves to me a little better instead of wasting all that breath just saying the same things over and over? I can't really answer any of these questions to the degree I want but trying has taken me on a marvelous journey.

I started this venture almost certain that I could set everyone straight, get rid of all those misgivings, half-truths, and inventions. I wanted my children and grandchildren to know how it really was, who their parents and grandparents were and, along the way, as a bonus, I could find out who my own father actually was.

I don't mean to imply that my mother didn't know. She did. I only knew his name and kind of remembered him from my early childhood. He had a pleasant face. I had stayed with him a time or two and had a few vague memories and two or three vivid ones, just moments. I knew that he had dated my half-sister, Mardie, something she herself told me was the one thing in her life she was ashamed of. And I later learned that during that same period he had been providing an apartment for the woman who became his third wife while he was living in the beautiful home of his second wife. And I knew he was a compulsive gambler and had a bad temper.

I guess I was looking for something good about him, some reason that five years after I was born Mother wrote in her journal that she alone knew him and loved him. And I wanted to know why in 1963, the year he died, when Mother was 79, I found her standing by a window in my apartment, moving a small snapshot in the light, tipping her head back, straining to see him, and saying, so softly, "Poor Chaunce."

As I launched into the history, my first important discovery was how much I had it wrong. My "truths" were built out of scraps pieced together from the scraps that others had pieced together. Previously I had thought of the pieces as shards, having substance, which, if I found the rest of them, could be reassembled into a recognizable whole.

I infer this to be the state of human knowledge in general. If it is true that nature itself cannot abide a vacuum, then it may also be true that human nature cannot. Given any number of scattered facts and memories, we have to fill in the blank spaces in some way that satisfies our own worldview. Having done so, we forget that we were just taking a wild stab at it in the first place and taking it for the truth. For example, sixty years ago, Auntie told me that Mother's first husband, Dr. William Eikner, whom she described as "the richest man in Nebraska," had shot a man he found sleeping with my mother. For the next forty years I wondered if "shot" equaled "killed." I decided to find out. About fifteen years ago I went to the Box Butte County Courthouse in Alliance, Nebraska, to see for myself. There was no record of either a shooting or altercation, just a number of cases in which the doctor had been the plaintiff attempting to collect his fees. Leaving the courthouse, I concluded that I should have asked my aunt for more information.

Still, the fill-in-the-blank view of human knowledge suits me just fine because it fits with my general belief that we human beings don't know as much about anything as we think we do, and that just as soon as we think we've found the answer to something we discover that we have, in fact, raised a whole new set of questions. I was trying to tell the Truth, but I was continually fabricating in order to make sense of the little bit of information I could glean.

However, the more times I discovered a fact that altered my previous understanding, the closer I felt to the experience itself. I found myself lost in time and then surprised to find myself now—a tired old woman, sitting here and in my comfortable old chair, squinting at the computer screen—while both the clock and my stomach tell me I have (only just) missed my lunch.

The age of the internet makes it remarkably easy to verify facts and to find evidence for almost any view of any object. Because my father enjoyed his fifteen minutes of fame as a writer-director in the early 1930s, when the film industry was a fledgling, I had no trouble finding appraisals, both positive and negative, of his work. I have to smile at the notion that he is most often remembered as being "largely forgotten."

The real trouble came in trying to decide who among his contemporaries or my own can say who the "real" Rowland Brown was. I never would have resolved this issue to my satisfaction had not Liz, my eldest daughter, and I had a rather unsettling discussion of an incident in her childhood. At some point I realized that each of us is stuck with the mother, daughter, and self we have only been able to see from our particular range of perspectives. No matter how clear our vision, how informed, the angles can never exactly coincide. No one is wrong. Taken together, all of the angles, all of the hearsay, all of the rumors comprise the reality of mortals.

With that final revelation or delusion, I finally understood the folly of my search for Truth. Perhaps the only true nonfiction is life itself. In writing about my sister Juneau, I returned to trying fiction, believing one could write a thousand stories given the known facts.

Yet, I love the small insight that justifies both my joy in the mystery of existence and my comfort in a failed mission. In truth, I can't "tell it like it is or ever was"—and at the same time I'm not lying.

In short, I am writing about people I know almost nothing about, for the benefit of people who may not yet or, for that matter, ever, exist.

You will thank me for this.

Megan McClard

Somewhere in Colorado

To C———R—B.

If you should come,
When I am dead,
And bending down,
Should stroke my head,
And look at me, O
With that fierce tenderness
Then that of me which you possess
Would stir again to life,
My lips would part —
To breathe once more — your name
                    Sweetheart —

                    Wildon McKenzie.

Megan

She is like a flawless pearl
Brought from the shore of a golden day
With the light of a day that's past
and gone
Held still in the line of its rosy sheen,

Child of a dream, too sweet to last.
Echo of that Paradise, somehow lost
and past.

1927 HOLLYWOOD

Hearsay

I was born September 7, 1927, in Los Angeles, California. According to Auntie, my mother's younger sister, I spent the first eleven months of my life in the Hollywood Osteopathic Hospital where I was born. No, I was neither sick nor premature (unless one believes the gypsy who told Mother that I had been born thirty years too soon). Although my mother once told me that I had been allergic to her milk, I rather think it more likely that Mother was allergic to me.

Despite Mother's own assertion that "any woman who says she wanted more than one child is lying," I was her sixth child. In 1915, after the birth of her second, she had gone to her brother-in-law, Dr. N. A. Thompson, for birth control advice. He suggested a method of contraception, probably either a pessary or a harsh douche. Fifteen months later, she had twins, each weighing more than six pounds.

My Aunt Octavia who had given birth to a twelve-pound son in 1909, discovered she was pregnant again only a few months later. According to Mother, her sister went down to the creek near the "soddy" and chose a willow stick, which she peeled and whittled until it was "nice and smooth

Entry in my mother's diary where she refers to me as a "pearl." Above that, she has written a love poem to my father, CRB.

and sharp." She was successful in aborting the fetus, but she pierced her uterus and nearly died.

My own birth was long and harrowing. I was crosswise in the uterus, presenting an arm, meaning my mother endured hours of a brutal obstetrical procedure as the physicians tried to maneuver me so they could pull me out by my feet. The alternative would have been to decapitate me. When Mother recovered from Twilight Sleep, the anesthetic she received during the final stage of labor, she said, "The baby's dead, of course." She could not have been overjoyed with the answer. She remained in the hospital for over two weeks following my birth. Very soon afterward, according to Juneau's diary, Mother returned to Boulder, Colorado, to her husband and children there.

Mother remained married to Neil B. McKenzie until his death in 1934, so I was legally his child. I'm sure his choice not to deny his paternity was due more to a desire to avoid the scandal in the then small community of Boulder than to acquire some other man's child as an heir. He did however invite his errant wife to bring me home to 809 Pine Street in Boulder. She chose not to, and I am most grateful to her for this. That was a house of sorrow.

I don't know anything about my mother's actual relationship with my father, Chauncey Rowland Brown, beyond knowing that Mother was crazy in love with him, and that he always seemed to be involved in concurrent affairs. His niece, Moya, thought of Mother as his secretary; possibly he did too. However, my mother thought of herself as his partner, his mistress, the one person who actually understood him and could save him from himself.

There is no way of confirming what either of my parents considered as a permanent solution for my care, but I'm pretty sure Mother expected my father to assume financial responsibility for me. Their temporary solution was to leave me in the hospital where I was born.

When Auntie first told me I had been left in the hospital for eleven months, I thought she was mistaken. I couldn't imagine what circumstances would allow parents to leave a healthy baby in the hospital for any time at all. But I was thinking of the mid-century hospitals where my own children were born. What seems unthinkable now might have been a relatively humane practice before the development of the many social services we have become accustomed to. I don't think it was abandonment; I think it was a last resort.

Do infants survive in iron cribs with starched nurses feeding them at arms' length for all that time? Perhaps some soft-breasted woman, with no nurse's badge, and no starch, picked me up and held me, thought fleetingly of adopting me. The facts don't matter, because no one on earth remembers them, and the truth is that I survived.

By 1931, my father, Chauncey Brown, had pretty much destroyed a promising career as a director. I can't even say whether he was motivated by high mindedness or egomania. Most commentators of the time thought it was simple temperament. Whatever it was, it apparently interfered with his feeling any obligation toward his children, his domestic partners, his

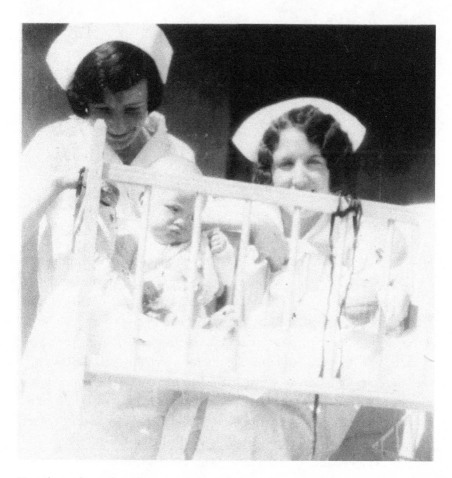

Me at about eight months, with nurses at the hospital, circa 1928

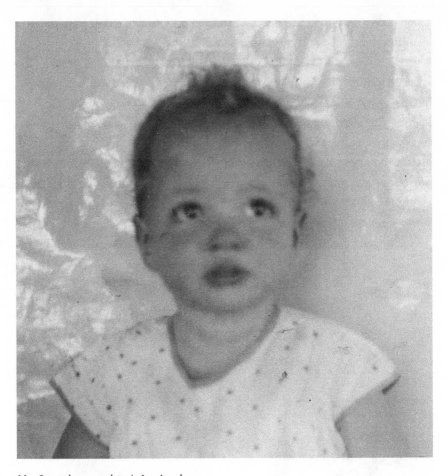

Me, 18 months, somewhere in Los Angeles

employers, or the cast and crew of the films he abandoned. According to his eldest son, Rowland C. W. Brown, born in 1923, his first wife left him because he had either been unable or unwilling to pay the obstetrical bills. He had a public reputation of having walked out on more films than he directed. He often refused to sign contracts with studios, allegedly because he didn't want to be tied to a working situation he didn't like. Ultimately, the producers found an advantage in the lack of a contract and fired him after he had done the lion's share of directing a film and gave the credit to another director, one, who in turn brought greater prestige to the product.

I remember several visits with Mrs. Maytham, my father's mother. At the time, I had no idea who she was or what claim she had on me. At least once I stayed overnight. At bedtime, she released the braid from its coiled bun, allowing her hair to cascade in blonde waves that flowed to her waist. Her sudden transformation frightened me; it was as though she had suddenly become another person. Another time, Hannah Maytham appeared at the Woods' on Christmas morning. If the Woods were expecting her, they didn't tell me. She drove me across town to her apartment in the Garden of Allah. There was a man there whom I knew as Chaunce, and Jack, a boy in knickers. Jack was playing with a mechanical horse race.

I watched the tiny horses race around the track, itching to play with it but I doubt that I asked. In my mind, nothing that I had ever received for Christmas came close to those racing horses. The track is the very first thing that I imagined I wanted but didn't get. Of course, I had no idea at all what a horse race was. (I had never been left in the car all day while my father gambled away the household money at Santa Anita as, many years later, my half-brother Steven, told me he had).

Just a few years ago I found the script for a screenplay Mother wrote in 1931 depicting an older woman and her former lover, a young screenwriter. He had a little shrine in his apartment with a picture of their child, whom he described as a pearl, a jewel. (Mother liked the term, perhaps invented it, and wrote a poem in which she asserted my flawless pearliness.) He promised that the little princess would be driven around town in her own Rolls Royce—someday. Meanwhile, he visited the adorable little creature daily in the hospital.

According to my half-sisters, Margery and Cynthia, after Mother returned to Boulder, she spent many sleepless nights, pacing the floor, smoking one cigarette after another. I, on the other hand, slept well in the foster home I lived in from the time I was twenty-one months old. Mother once told me that although my foster home was far from ideal, she knew that I was well nourished and that my foster parents were decent people.

I remember very few events before I was three years old, but I remember visiting my mother, Alwilda McKenzie, in a hotel room several times. I remember the room, but don't know whether she remained at the same hotel or whether she moved from place to place. I remember a pull-down bed, Palmolive soap, a filmy window. Mother called me "Darling" and smoked cigarettes from a green fifty-flat box (Luckies). Once, there were two or three other women there. They were smoking and one of their cigarettes brushed my arm, burning it slightly. I was indignant. It could have been the same visit that Mother sang "Baby's Boat's A Silver Moon," although she must have sung it to me many more times than once as I lay beside her in bed, because, when I had my own babies, I knew the words: "Sail baby sail/Out on that sea/Only don't forget to sail/Back again to me."

Me, riding a pony on an outing, circa 1930

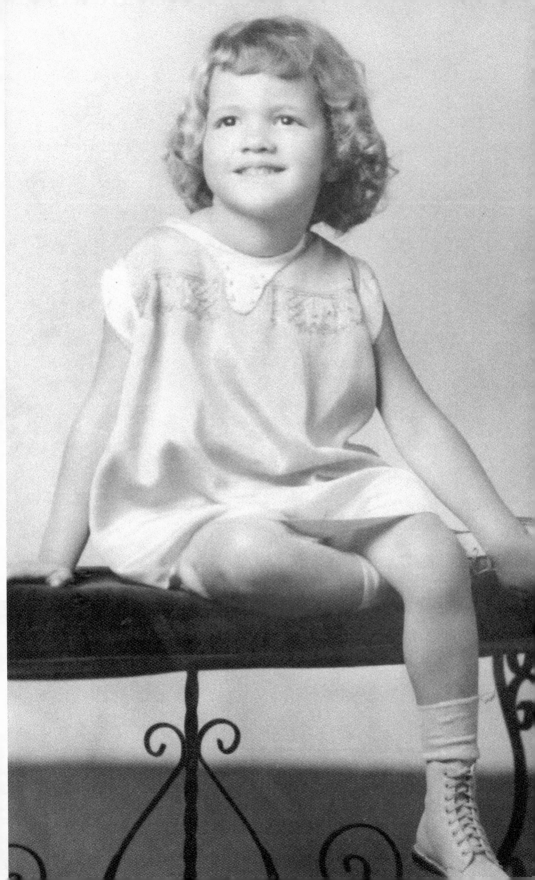

1929 To the Woods

"In This World but Not of This World"

"We've had Megan with us since she was twenty-one months old," Mrs. Wood would repeat to visitors, because she always had to explain me. The explanation would always remind me that I didn't really belong in the little white house with its two absolutely symmetrical palm trees, and I would feel vaguely ashamed. I had to remember that I was somehow related to "That Woman" who seemed to appear from nowhere sometimes to take me away from the little house.

Mrs. Wood was a very responsible person, kind but not demonstrative. She was strict; her house was orderly. The flowers in her yard were planted in straight rows, and she kept their beds weeded and bug-free. Few hugs or kisses, no sitting on a lap to be read to, no endearing pet names. Mrs. Wood called DeLoris, her adopted daughter, Dee, but always called me Megan. The entire time I stayed with the Woods, I slept on a cot in DeLoris's room at the end of a big oak double bed, probably displaced when Mr. and Mrs. Wood decided they would be more comfortable sleeping in twin beds.

But I always had the necessities: clean clothes that had been washed on Monday and ironed on Tuesday, and a breakfast of oatmeal, served

Me, in Los Angeles, around three years old

1122 West Seventieth Street, Los Angeles where, according to the 1930 Census, I was "Meegan" McKenzie, a two-and-half-year-old lodger

shortly after Mr. Wood had backed out of the driveway on his way to work. Dinner was meat, potatoes, usually boiled or baked and served with canned peas and carrots, canned beets, canned green beans, or freshly shelled peas cooked until they were the same color as canned peas. It was on the table at five thirty. If there was dessert, it was red Jell-O. Later, when I went to school, lunch was a peanut butter or American cheese sandwich, wrapped in wax paper, an apple, and a thermos of milk packed the night before and tucked into a lunch box. In addition, I had a spoonful of cod liver oil every day, a dose of milk of magnesia every Saturday, and at least a couple of doses of castor oil a year. I received a weekly bath and an annual enema.

Although she was the guardian of my health, the only time I remember going to a doctor was the trip to the neighborhood chiropractor when I was burned. Although Mrs. Wood had been vaccinated for smallpox and had a nickel-sized scar to show for it, she would not sign the permission slips for the required free vaccinations at school, always writing a note explaining that my mother was a Christian Scientist and did not believe in vaccination. Except for the prescribed purgatives, Mrs. Wood herself had more faith in prayer than modern medicine.

From the time I went to live with Edna and William Wood, I don't remember a meal that didn't begin with a simple giving of thanks for the food we ate. The Woods didn't "say grace," but something like, "Dear Lord, we thank you for this food and all of the blessings you have given us today. In Jesus' name. Amen." I never doubted that God was listening. I never wondered how he could distinguish Mrs. Wood's thin voice in the perpetual hum of requests rising from Earth. Nor did I question the importance of my own nightly prayers before crawling into bed. How could I? Mrs. Wood often reminded me of the dangers of forgetting to say them. She spoke of a dear little boy she knew who forgot to say his prayers just once and died of pneumonia before he had a chance to ask for forgiveness, and another little boy who told his mean mother, "You'll be sollow. I won't be he' tomollow," and then, apparently by simply omitting his prayers, went to sit eternally at Jesus' side.

Jesus was ever-present. I think every room except the bathroom had either a picture of hazel-eyed Jesus, or some other reminder. (Now when I see the popular print I remember from childhood, I notice He seems to be looking off into space as though He's deliberately trying to avoid eye contact.) I liked the small phosphorescent cross that nestled among the white bows imprinted on the sky-blue wallpaper of DeLoris's room, the one I shared. I have a feeling it was something DeLoris bought on my behalf, something I even asked for, this thing that absorbed light all day and glowed green at night.

And there was music in the house. As she did the dishes, Mrs. Wood sang hymns in a high, thin voice. Sometimes she just hummed, but I don't remember Mrs. Wood ever singing or humming anything but hymns. For my foster mother, religion was neither a passing persuasion nor a ritual attended on Sunday; it was the way things were. Without question.

"Jesus was ever-present.... He seems to be looking off into space as though He's deliberately trying to avoid eye contact."

I don't think church taught her to fear so much of the world she lived in. Maybe it was the de facto segregation imposed by the doctrine of Christians being "in this world but not of this world," but my foster mother disliked those who were not like her. For example, she was terrified of "Niggers." It surprised me to learn that when DeLoris was seven or eight years old, the Woods had moved to another school district because Mrs. Wood saw Dee holding a little Black schoolmate's hand as they walked home from school. There were no Black children at my school. The only Blacks I ever saw were groups of Gospel singers who sometimes performed at church, who were loved there and seemed to be celebrated.

Mrs. Wood said Jews were "God's chosen people," but she was always suspicious of them. She didn't call the peddlers "rag sheenies" as some did, but she made sure to mention the grocers' Jewish or Japanese decent, or that the butcher was Italian. Her very dearest friends were the Knittles who were converts to the Church of Nazarene, and therefore acceptable, being "Christian Jews." She did say that Roman Catholics "weren't Christians," and openly disliked them. I think in her mind, the Pope was the Antichrist. Maybe she was ambivalent about Methodists and Presbyterians, but more tolerant because she felt they meant well and aspired to be her definition of Christian.

I say, "she" because although Mr. Wood sat beside her every Sunday and tithed, he never claimed salvation of any degree. He was a small stakes sinner. He smoked enough Camels to have yellow stains on his fingers, and sometimes came home late from work to accusations of having liquor on his breath. When Mrs. Wood sang "Will There Be Any Stars In My Crown?" over the sink, from the living room, her husband would counter in a husky bass, "No, not one, no not one."

"Oh, Billy!" she would say.

I was "Christianized" early in life although I was never actually reborn. I'm not sure what happened but I remain unregenerate to this day. To tell the truth, I was never too keen on the idea of getting myself saved, but always enjoyed Sunday School, the nice pictures and stickers for memorizing Bible verses. By the time I was six and sent to Billings I had memorized the Lord's Prayer and the Twenty-third Psalm, and was particularly fond of the latter. I could just see those three little girls, "Shirley, Goodness, and Mercy," giggling as they trailed along behind the brave shepherd boy who carried a slingshot in his back pocket.

And of course, when I was younger, like everyone, I loved Baby Jesus because he always showed up right before the actual Christmas when Sandy Claws managed to visit Los Angeles without being detected. All of those things were very nice, but I didn't like the sin talk and The Ten Commandments gave me the heebie-jeebies. I didn't even know what some of those things were that might cause me to end up in Hell.

I didn't like either of the two church services I went to every Sunday. In the first place, the seats were very uncomfortable. I was a skinny child and my tailbone used to hurt from sitting too long on wooden seats. We

Edna Wood, circa 1945

went to a Baptist Church for a short time and a Christian Church for an
even shorter time, but the Foursquare Church dominated my early
childhood and the Full Gospel Church shaped my early adolescence.
The Foursquare Church we attended was all hellfire and brimstone. The
preacher, Brother Lee, yelled warnings of the Second Coming and
Judgment Day. Brother Lilly, the pastor of the Full Gospel Church that
the Woods finally settled into, was quieter. He focused on God's love and the
rewards awaiting the born-again in heaven. He told us that someday we
would sit by Jesus' side. I would have to say that I never found the honor
of sitting beside Jesus forever and ever especially appealing. I now hope
that the pastor's reward was seeing his six-year-old daughter, restored,
running happily toward him, uninterrupted by the car that skidded,

brakes screeching between them. I will always remember John Bunyon Lilly as a sweet and gentle shepherd.

Mrs. Wood was not only a "Sunday Christian"; her religion was her life. Mother Wood was also Sister Wood, one of Sister Aimee's Lighthouse Workers, who volunteered to clean the houses of invalids, visit the sick, and look after the needy who were stranded in the wake of the Great Depression. She wore a uniform that resembled an army nurse's uniform: a starched white dress, a dark necktie embellished with a lighthouse, and topped with a navy-blue cape.

We spent hot summer days driving around Los Angeles in an Essex automobile that started with a crank. I, sitting in the backseat, sick from fumes and heat and boredom, remember watching Sister Wood and

Me with Mr. and Mrs. Wood in San Francisco, 1935

another Lighthouse Worker carry bags of donated food into house after dreary house every week. Often, after what seemed at least one full eternity, the two women emerged, shaking their heads and muttering about filth under the sink, moldy gravy in the icebox, and plugged toilets; in the car, they half whispered words like *bedsores*, *milk leg*, and *sugar diebeetus*. If I learned anything from their post-visit conversations, it was that I didn't ever want to set foot in the houses they entered. I hated the less fortunate, whoever they were. Thankfully, one evil habit I never developed was doing good.

The high points of my childhood encounter with religion were attending several of Brother Parrott's tent revivals. Of course, the tent itself promised fun and, in my memory, it still far outshines the Barnum and Bailey. For one thing, it smelled better than a circus. The wood shavings were still fragrant, unsullied by man or beast. The music was familiar; I could sing along with my favorites and clap to the familiar rhythms of those I didn't know. The service was joyful. People shouted "Hallelujah!" It was a party atmosphere: "Gimme that old time religion!" In contrast, the circus I later saw in Billings, Montana, was largely disappointing. Clowns were supposed to be funny, but to a six-year-old they were more puzzling. I thought their yarn hair was funny—odd funny, not happy funny.

Now I understand that the Barnum & Bailey Circus also had elements of Old Testament religion. The lion tamers and elephant trainers, the

Above: Aimee Semple McPherson, flanked by Lighthouse Workers, circa 1930
Left: Aimee Semple McPherson in front of her "gospel car" Source: Pentacostal Archives

circus itself, with its train of caged and humbled animals, demonstrated
the superiority of man and his likeness to his creator:

> And God said, Let us make man in our image, after
> our likeness: and let them have dominion over the
> fish of the sea, and over the fowl of the air, and over
> the cattle, and over all the earth, and over every
> creeping thing that creepeth upon the earth. (Genesis 1:25)

Brother Parrott's tent show was more New Testament. It featured
salvation, forgiveness, and miraculous healing. The Reverend Parrott could
lay his hands on the head of someone's widowed grandmother—so sick that
her son had to push her wheelchair down the aisle over the wood

APPEARING HERE

REV. EVERETT B. PARROTT

Evangelist Opens Meetings Sunday

Rev. Everett B. Parrott, for 25 years a traveling evangelist, will open a series of meetings at 7:30 p.m. Sunday at the Assembly of God Church, 1749 East Broadway. He will be assisted by Rev. and Mrs. Theodore Brocke.

Services will be held daily at 10 a.m. and 7:30 p.m. Rev. and Mrs. Brocke will have charge of the morning services. Reverend Parrott was for ten years a Methodist conference evangelist before going into the general evangelistic field. He has held revivals in large cities, such as Atlanta, Ga., and St. Louis.

He usually holds his meetings in a large tent, but Tucson nights are too chilly for tent services. The meetings will be held indoors.

LIFE STORY

Mrs. Everett B. Parrott, be-low, wife of the evangelist, will tell her life story as a feature of the revival program in the Big Tent Cathedral at First street and Orange avenue tonight.

Mrs. Everett B. Parrott, wife of the evangelist now conducting revival meetings at First street and Orange avenue, will tell her life story at the Big Tent Cathedral tonight, it is announced.

Her narrative, telling how she came to join the Parrott revival party, is heralded as one of the most interesting features of the campaign thus far.

An ardent co-worker with her husband, Mrs. Parrott is regarded as an able song director, leading the revival singing nightly; also giving scriptural instruction to those desiring the evangelist's prayer for healing, it is said.

The Rev. Mr. Parrott will preach another prophetic sermon Thursday evening at 7:30 entitled, "The March of the Dictators." He will show how the use of dictators in various nations today is a literal fulfillment of Bible prophecy.

shavings—and she would spring from the chair, arms raised toward heaven, and shout "Hallelujah!" It was wonderful to see. Grandma would then sit back down and her son would push her back up the aisle as she wept into a wadded handkerchief. Who knew whether or not her faith had failed her?

Most often, I was too short to see any evidence of the miracle and would have to ask DeLoris or Mother Wood what had happened. One of them would answer, "He had fits," or "She had a tumor as big as a watermelon. It disappeared." One time, I think it was DeLoris who said, "It fell on the floor." I wished that I had been tall enough to see for myself. In my own mind, a "toomer" was a big beige, liquid-filled balloonish thing. Slimy. I supposed it had made a wonderful splash.

Left: various newspaper clippings. Top: from Los Angeles Times 1936. Everett Parrott and his wife, Myrtle Kuhlmann Parrott were fixtures on the tent revival circuit. Their last name was memorable.

1933 CHAUNCE RESCUES ME

I must have been waiting most of my life for someone to rescue me. I think my idea of "father" was based on "My Father Who Art in Heaven," that all-powerful but invisible daddy of us all who made me, wrote all those rules that I shalt obey, watched me constantly, forgave my sins (as long as they were not unforgivable), and promised to rescue me even if I were swallowed by a whale. I had actually seen my earthly, rather fleshy father several times—and on at least one occasion he *had* rescued me. Though I didn't know at the time that he was my father or that I even had an earthly father. Way back when he was just a nice man named Chaunce.

I only knew him from a couple of encounters on the bridge of time between September 7, 1927, and April 6, 1963. The first time, I was visiting the woman Mrs. Maytham, who, at the time, could have been a fairy godmother or a witch. I didn't like her especially, even though she had once made me a delicious liver loaf. (She was, in fact, his mother.)

The day Chaunce rescued me, I had inadvertently locked myself in Mrs. Maytham's bathroom at her Garden of Allah apartment. I probably would have been perfectly comfortable hanging out there for the entire visit had I not flushed the toilet and set off a flood that felt like it would

Garden of Allah, circa 1936

last until a dove flew in with an olive branch. I went "berserk." As Mrs. Maytham pleaded with me, telling me just to turn the something-something that was right above the something on the door, Chaunce appeared, godlike, feet first through a bathroom window, walked on the water, took my hand and led me through the door that swung open before us.

I must have liked Chaunce. I don't remember having any negative feelings toward him as I did about the other strangers in my early childhood: my mother, my grandmother, and my aunt. I built my father from small, scattered scraps, few of which were remnants of the genuine article. My personal contact with him included the rescue from the toilet tsunami; the way his checked pant leg fit his thigh as I sat next to him in the front seat of a car; being with him and Mother at Laguna, he warning me not to sit on a round cactus that I mistook for a "tuffet"; staying with him and a dark-haired woman I knew as "Aunt Marcella." (When I was an adult, my mother had asked me if I remembered my Aunt Jean, Chaunce's sister. I told her the only aunt I remembered was Marcella. Mother snapped, "Marcella was *not* your aunt.")

Mother was my major source of the stuff I made into a father. She said that when Chaunce arrived at an otherwise lifeless event, "the party began." According to Mother, he was a genius; he was a son-of-a-bitch; he had dropped out of Harvard; he had joined the Navy when he was sixteen but "was sent home when they discovered his age." He was "good looking." He had broad shoulders. Strong. He was a boxer. She said that as Jack Dempsey's sparring partner he had once knocked him down. When I was eighteen and pregnant with Michael, she told me that if Chaunce had known about my husband's behavior, "He would have broken his jaw."

She referred to him as a director, famous for walking out on John Barrymore, who regularly drank "a quart of whiskey a day." Mother claimed that Chaunce had both written and directed *Angels with Dirty Faces* but had been replaced as director in the last week, in favor of Michael Curtiz, who had been credited with directing four other films that year. Mother said that Chaunce regularly lost huge sums of money at Santa Anita. "He would get a check from the studio and head for the track."

I remember quite vividly Mother taking me into a dark, noisy studio to be in the 1931 version of *Daddy Long Legs.* My foster mother must have

Portrait of my father as a young man, circa 1918

cautioned me about the evils of the place because, according to Mother,
I balked as we entered, tugging and crying, "Jesus doesn't want me to go in
here." On the set, in my one scene, I was an extra orphan. (Talk about
typecasting!) The movie was panned, possibly because the director didn't
recognize method acting and had no appreciation of my interpretation of
a frightened and abandoned four-year-old. Actually, I think my film debut
ended up on the cutting room floor. Within months, Shirley Temple tap-
danced her way into America's heart and made her parents rich.

* * *

Me, age four, with Ching, circa 1932

* * *

When I was all grown up, my mother's sister Octavia, whom I called
Auntie, informed me that the darling, fluffy puppy and red tricycle given
to me anonymously when I was a toddler had both come from Chaunce.
I surmised that she had been the go-between. Mr. Wood said the tricycle
was a really good one because it had ball bearings. I was allowed to ride it
at full speed from the back porch to the backyard gate, a distance of at
least forty feet. The fluffy puppy turned out to be a one-person dog, a
Chow bitch we called Ching, whose black tongue dripped as she lay on
the back porch in front of the screen door, guarding Mrs. Wood.

My sister Mardie, who visited me several times in Los Angeles after we left Billings, added more scraps to my paternal assemblage. According to my mother, Mardie was lunching with a friend at the Brown Derby one day when a man approached her, "Alwilda?" The meeting was a remarkable and unlikely coincidence: I suspect Mother's main point in telling me about it was that Chaunce had mistaken her twenty-five-year-old daughter Mardie for an ageless Alwilda. Mother also loved quoting Mardie, who said that my father was "attractive—in a repulsive sort of way."

According to Mother, this chance encounter led to Mardie and Chaunce developing an ongoing dialogue about his sending me to Flintridge Academy, a girls' boarding school in La Cañada founded by Dominican nuns. During that same trip, Mardie visited me at the Woods'. After only a few minutes, she invited me to go with her to have a "chocolate short." But instead of going directly to the drugstore soda fountain we sat in Mardie's car for a time and talked about what I was studying at Horace Mann Junior High School, and what I wanted to be. I'm sure I told her I was taking art and that my poster of an elf sitting under a mushroom, "Shelter the Needy," had won third place in the Los Angeles Community Chest contest. Years later, I learned that the real purpose of the car conversation was to allow my father, blocked from contact with me by a restraining order, a chance to see me as he stood at the end of the block.

When I was sixteen, by then living in Denver with Mother, I learned that Mardie and Chaunce had done a great deal more than talk about my attending Flintridge. Mardie was driving at record-setting speed on the road to Boulder. I was sitting in the front seat and two of Mardie's friends who had gone to California with her in the early forties were in the back. Someone behind me said, "Mardie, what ever happened to that smooth guy you were seeing, the one with the beautiful house in Beverly Hills?" Mardie nearly drove off the road, but the woman continued, "What was his name? Chaunce?" Perhaps twenty years later, Mardie, blurry-eyed from bourbon, said that she had done only one thing in her life that she was ashamed of. Without filling in the big blank, she said, "Please don't ever tell Mother."

I know much of what my father did and what he didn't do. He left a paper trail and, now, a digital one. He also left at least five offspring—his essence, his mark, his actual protoplasm, and his broken promises.

Because I have had to reconstruct him, I probably know more about Rowland Brown than I might have had I been distracted by his presence.

A month or so after his death, his widow, Karen, sent me an unfinished letter, writ small on pinkish, laid paper with a fine-nibbed pen. He'd started it over a year before his death, a response to my plea for money so I could leave my husband. The letter began, "I wondered how long it would take you to escape Alwilda's clutch and contact me," followed by a discussion of my mother's considerable shortcomings. He wrote that, a few years back, Mardie had shown some concern about my situation in the foster home and they had discussed the possibility of sending me to a boarding school but at the time he was married to "a girl from New Orleans," and it wasn't.... His handwriting shriveled, each line smaller than the last; unreadable, it trailed into a wriggling line.

I treasured the letter as evidence of both my father's existence and my own. I tucked it away in a secure place—I think between the pages of some wonderful novel I imagined I would keep forever but subsequently sold at a garage sale. But I still search for it now and then.

* * *

Today, I decided to go through my accordion letter file one more time. I looked under B, where I found a bundle of letters from Carolyn DiPalma and a postcard from Danni Lederman. Then I reached into the thickest file and found an assortment, some held together with a rubber band, some wrapped in paper labeled "students, etc." His thin letter was among the cetera, all but invisible. I have appended a copy. Its content will reveal me as an unreliable narrator, along with all the others. That is, the handwriting on the second page doesn't flatline at all. It returns to normal. The paper isn't laid but I think I see a pinkish tinge in the portion that hasn't yellowed. He doesn't mention the school but he does refer to the dresses and slippers he sent from Paris, the dresses I remember hanging, unworn, in my closet at Mrs. Wood's. I have no memory of the slippers.

My father, fishing

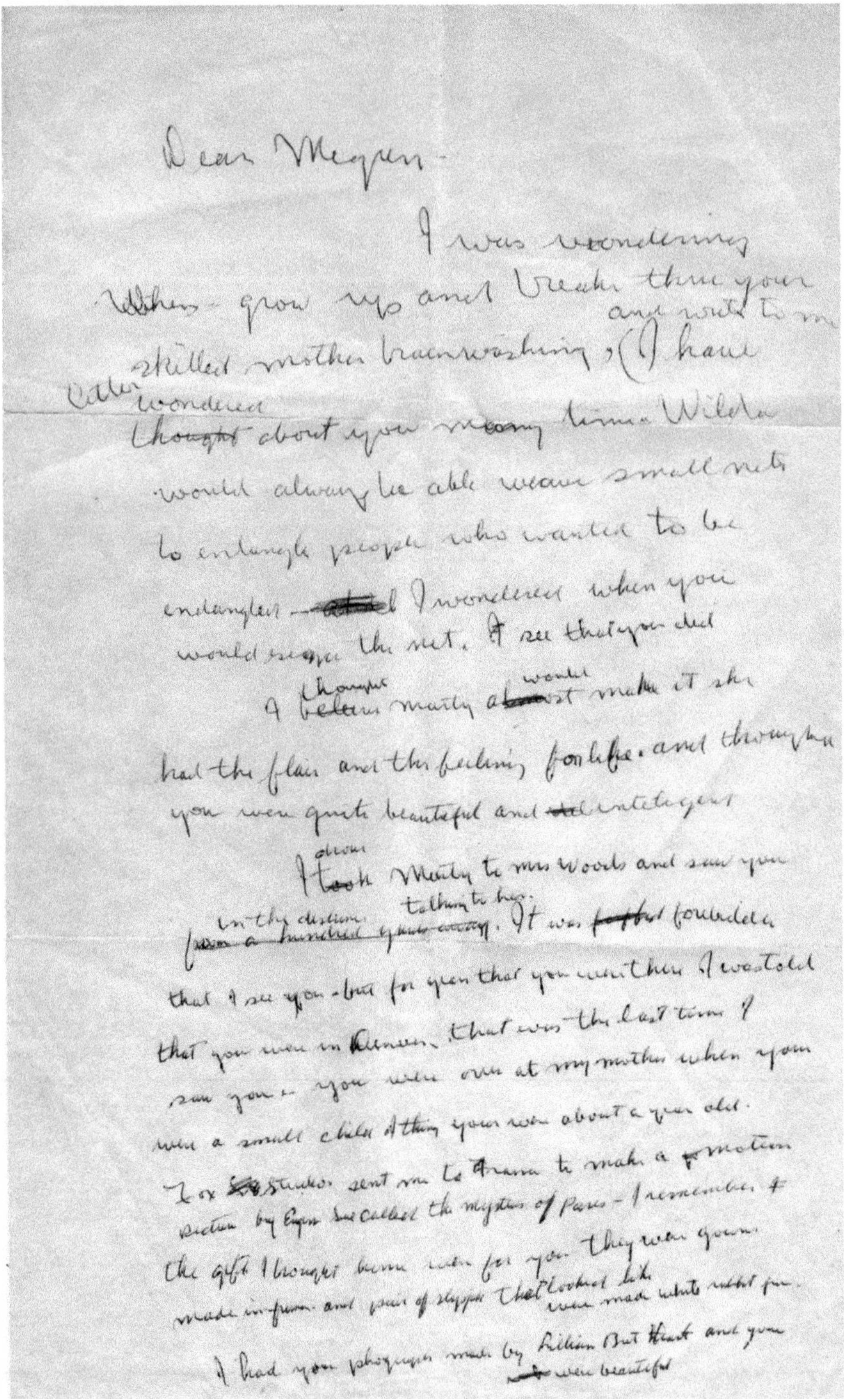

Dear Megun—

I was wondering
when you grow up and break through your
skilled mother brainwashing, (I have
wondered
thought about you many times. Wilda
would always be able weave small nets
to entangle people who wanted to be
entangled — and I wondered when you
would escape the net. I see that you did

I believe Marily almost would make it she
had the flair and the feeling for life. and I thought
you were quite beautiful and intelligent

I took Marily to mrs woods and saw you
in the distance talking to her.
from a hundred years away. It was founded
that I see you — but for years that you went there I was told
that you were in Denver. that was the last time I
saw you — you were over at my mothers when you
were a small child I think you were about a year old.

Fox studios sent me to France to make a motion
picture by Eugene sue called the mystery of Paris — I remember. +
the gift I brought home were for you. They were gowns
made in france and pair of slippers that looked like
were made white rabbit fur
I had your photograph made by Lillian But Kurt and you
were beautiful

Letter from my father found in my accordion file

40 | LEAVINGS

My Mother wanted to adopt you but
Wilda would not have any part of my mother
and my mother would not have any part of wilda
—— so you d——— disappeared
until Mary came to Hollywood with two other
girls from Boulder ⹀ I was married about that
time to a girl from New Orleans

1932 - 33 No Kindergarten

I remember several moments from my fifth birthday party. We were at a picnic table in a park. Mother Wood had baked me a wonderful cake. It was a moist and heavy orange cake, the kind I still like, but the kind Mother Wood always apologized for, a fallen cake. Her cakes always fell—through no fault of her own—but because someone had walked too heavily. Or run, or even jumped on the kitchen floor while the cake was in the oven. On top of that fortunately fallen cake were poised five frosted animal crackers, as though ready to bob up and down on my merry-go-round.

My memory of the cake has far outlasted all but one of the guests. It may be that when I die, the last crumb of that cake will fade with me— as will that nasty little boy with dirty, sticky hands. I don't think I had ever seen him before. DeLoris, my foster sister, was taking care of him for the afternoon. I have no idea what his mouth looked like, or whether his nose needed a good wiping or his shoes needed tying, but that disgusting little hand has stayed with me for seventy-seven years, grasping what I think was an elephant cookie with a smudge of orange frosting.

My fifth birthday party, 1932

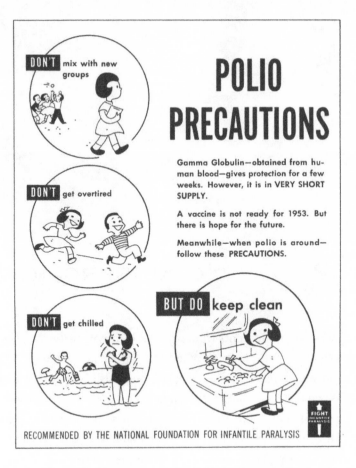

Posters like this 1953 one were plentiful during the 1934 outbreak

I remember one other fragment of that boy: the funny little thing that looked to me like a thumb made of gristle. DeLoris pointed to it when I went with them to the park bathrooms. As he held it over the rim of the toilet, she explained, "That's what little boys make a brookie with!"

Other kids went to kindergarten when they were five but Mother Wood decided against sending me. I don't know why. Maybe it was fear of my getting a disease. The polio epidemic didn't come to Los Angles until 1934, but it was always around, and I was not immunized against smallpox or diphtheria either. Mother Wood chose against it, using my mother's religion as her excuse, even though California schools required that children be immunized against these diseases and even though I know for a fact that I got immunized immediately on my arrival in Billings when I was seven and again on my arrival in Denver when I was fifteen.

During my entire childhood, poliomyelitis (we called it infantile paralysis then) was endemic in Southern California. Because of polio, kids had to take afternoon naps, swimming pools were closed during the hottest months, beaches were quarantined and houseflies demonized. (I doubted flies were guilty of more than rather indiscriminate taste but supposedly they carried whatever it was that caused polio by one minute craving dog poop and the next peanut butter and jelly or cooling their feet and relieving themselves on a scoop of strawberry ice cream.)

Whatever the reason, I stayed home that year while other children I knew went to kindergarten. Namyra Withers went and I was jealous of her, of her opportunity to learn. She lived across the street, and before she started school at times we both might sit on our respective curbs and fight about something, usually about whose tortoise it was that had wandered first into my yard and then into hers.

Though I was eager to go to school I didn't mind or even notice the solitary nature of my activities that year. I was taken by every trail of ants, every blade of grass. I didn't need other children yet, because I was suspicious of their encroachments and usurpations. I couldn't know that the main thing children learn in kindergarten is how to share and how to enjoy other children.

Two big events occurred in March of 1933, near the end of the school year: my burn, and the earthquake. I got burned by being disobedient. I was supposed to sit on the porch while Mr. Wood was using a gasoline torch to clean the stove burners. I wanted so badly to see that, really up close. I sat for as long as I could before very quietly sitting on an upturned flowerpot, right behind Mr. Wood. I don't think he knew I was there at all. Almost immediately, a gusty wind came up and a ball of fire engulfed us and caught my skirt and socks on fire. I ran, terrified. People were yelling at me to lie down and roll on the grass and that made no sense at all. Why would I lie down? Mother Wood came out and I ran toward her. She grabbed me and wrapped me in her apron, which put the flames out. She took me into the kitchen and rubbed olive oil on my burns. It was so horribly painful, all over my legs. It was so bad that the Woods took me to the doctor, a chiropractor, who continued to do

Los Angeles earthquake damage, 1933, postcard image

painful things to me. I felt punished, sure that God had used nature to punish me for being disobedient.

When the Long Beach earthquake struck on March 10, 1933, the initial shock must have wakened me from a dream, because I thought it was just my foster sister bumping against my cot as she got out of bed. (I remember the date because, as I later learned, March 10 was my mother's birthday.) I was puzzled when she and my foster mother appeared at the bedroom door, telling me that I was all right and how they had struggled to keep their balance on the undulating floor. Mother Wood had slipped on a piece of china, her row of hand-painted, china plates now in shards on the dining-room floor. The upright player piano was in the middle of the living room. Kitchen cupboards had disgorged their Ball jars of tomatoes, peaches, and piccalilli, zinc-lidded glass intact.

Though just a shiver as earthquakes go, I remember its impact quite vividly. We were ordered to stay out of the house until we could be certain the gas lines were intact. When we were allowed back into the house, we kept our eyes on the little chains on the lamps. A jiggle signaled an impending aftershock. A few days later, Mr. Wood took the family on a drive to survey the damage. I was horrified, not by the thought of children left homeless, crushed, or dead, but by the possibility that a person (I, for instance) might have been sitting on the toilet when the bathroom wall fell away.

Brass blow torch like the one Mr. Wood was using to clean the stove burners

That year cemented some learning: not to disobey, that I should be afraid of houseflies, swimming pools and other children. I did not learn to overcome my natural curiosity.

Tent school in Los Angeles, 1933, Los Angeles Times Archive, UCLA

Coda

That was pretty minor damage in a quake that I later learned had killed 120 people and damaged or destroyed hundreds of masonry buildings, including 120 schools, seventy of which were demolished.

All of the schools built of reinforced concrete withstood the magnitude 6.4 shock. Had it occurred during school hours the casualties would have been much higher. Conversely, had it not occurred at all, it is likely that many more Californians would have lost their lives in subsequent, stronger earthquakes.

As a direct result of the structural failures of unreinforced masonry schools, earthquake-resistant design and construction were mandated for public schools: K-12 and community colleges. This was due largely to the efforts of California Assembly Member Charles Field, and the law, known as the Field Act, was passed on April 10, 1933. It and its subsequent revisions authorized the Division of Architecture of the California State Department of Works to review and approve all public school plans and specifications and to furnish general supervision of the construction work. No Field Act school has ever failed in an earthquake.

Eventually I benefited from both the earthquake and the Field Act. Shortly after my return from Billings I got to attend fourth grade in a tent while WPA—or was it PWA?— workers brought Raymond Avenue Grammar School up to the new standards. Later on I would understand the importance of the Works Projects Administration as an integral part of the American New Deal. I'm pretty sure they repaired that crack in the ceiling of Miss Schumacher's room first thing.

1933 First Grade

Ready or Not

I started first grade six months after the quake. Having heard rumors of unsafe school buildings and how many children would have been crushed or killed had school been in session, I worried. I realized that sitting at my desk when the ceiling fell down might be even worse than sitting on the toilet when the wall fell. Miss Schumacher's room was very nice and conveniently located right next to the entrance from the playground of Raymond Avenue Grammar School. There were interesting things to look at: lumpy families made from modeling clay stood in front of shoebox houses. Good Humor–stick fences marked boundaries. There was a grey street lined with lampposts, topped with white marbles. Those were a few of my favorite things.

I also loved the milk and graham crackers we had every morning. I had no idea they weren't a traditional school snack but a program established by the USDA in 1933 to make use of surplus grain and dairy products.

Most of all, I loved my desk. It had a place to put my pencil box and Crayolas. A private place. The desktop was smooth and cool. I liked the way it smelled when the teacher made us put our heads down for "rest time." But when my head was down and I had nothing better to do, I didn't

Me, at about age six, circa 1933

Jack set like the one that DeLoris gave me. Photo: Allison Livingston, the Pink Room

rest; I worried. I worried about recess. I worried about the big crack in the ceiling. Maybe I even cried.

Did I cry on the playground? It represented everything I wanted to be and do, that I had so looked forward to, and everything I felt somehow excluded from. I didn't know anyone's name and no one knew mine. At recess, when the first graders broke from the orderly line obediently formed in the hall before being released to run outside to their "play" stations, I was completely out of my element. The girls played hopscotch or jumped rope and chanted, "Down by the ocean, down by the sea, Johnny broke a bottle and blamed it on me." The boys raced, yelling, and laughing, toward the swings and slides. Some played ball. Some drew circles for marble games. They were used to playing games with each other.

I could recite "For God so loved the world that he gave his only begotten son," (whatever begotten meant), but I didn't know how to jump to it. I'd never even seen a long rope with a girl turning it at each end and another in the middle jumping. I watched the other kids having fun. They were so good at it.

Most of the children had known each other from kindergarten. They knew each other's names. Bobby, Billy, Tommy, Jack, Jimmy, and Henry were friends. Betty, Dorothy, Katherine, Jane, Nancy, Joan, and Suzanne took turns at jump rope. I was Megan, but Megan didn't mean anything to anybody. I hadn't learned about cooperation, only about obedience. I probably pouted and maybe whimpered.

DeLoris, who was in high school and knew everything about school (and some fascinating things about body parts), tried to help me fit in. She gave me a lagger, but it didn't come with a manual and I was terrible at throwing it. Whether or not any of the girls were much better than I was, I felt embarrassed. And for all of my hopping practice, I couldn't hop over anything. DeLoris even made me a bag for jacks in her sewing class and donated the jacks from her own grammar school days, but when two friendly little girls invited me to join them and I couldn't get past twosies, I felt defective. I hated school. It wasn't for me. I didn't have the wisdom of my future granddaughter, Zoë, who, when she was in kindergarten, already knew that "Ev'body's diffent!" I could have cried.

After two weeks Miss Schumacher agreed with Mrs. Wood, or vice versa, that I was not ready for school. Miss Schumacher could not have been too sorry to lose such a problem: clearly, to her, I was a spoiled only child, used to having my own way. Mrs. Wood wrote Mother that I was too standoffish. I couldn't get along with other children. At some point I was told or overheard someone say that at school I "wouldn't stop crying." I don't remember crying, but I do remember awful feelings of shame, fear, frustration, disappointment, and exclusion.

* * *

* * *

After that, I sat at home at my own small table in the Woods' kitchen. Or played alone in the Woods' backyard, counting how many times I could bounce a ball on a rubber band on its paddle, jumping off the back-porch steps, or (my favorite), watching ants wander into little bottles of ant poison, perched along the edge of the sidewalk. I never tired of watching the natural world—though I didn't get dirty. I could wear a dress all week, alternating one washed, starched, and ironed dress with another.

I didn't play with the neighborhood children much at all. They were "bad," that is, sinners. Some of them were Catholics. Some of them had runny noses. Some of them were even boys. Mrs. Wood let me play with Ruthie Chambers only once, and I liked her though she was a year younger than I. She wanted to play doctor. Mrs. Wood intuited that; she preferred I play with evil Namyra Withers, who lived across the street, kitty-corner to the left. Namyra's father was a policeman, the family Christian, and she loved baby dolls. I liked my dolls, but I did not love them.

I had outgrown the tricycle and Ching became ever more hostile and always made coming in from the outdoors an ordeal. "My dog" hated me, and I hated her and I was afraid of her. She growled fiercely every time I came to the screen door, imposing herself threateningly between me and Mrs. Wood—Mrs. Wood's territory. I had to wait for Mrs. Wood to come to the back door and let me pass. And Ching wasn't just putting on a show. She bit me several times.

A year that had started for me with great anticipation and excitement in going to school to learn ended up being the year I became aware of my unhappiness and my feeling of not belonging.

Me, age eight with DeLoris in San Francisco

Me with Eleanor, Mr. Wood's granddaughter, playing in yard

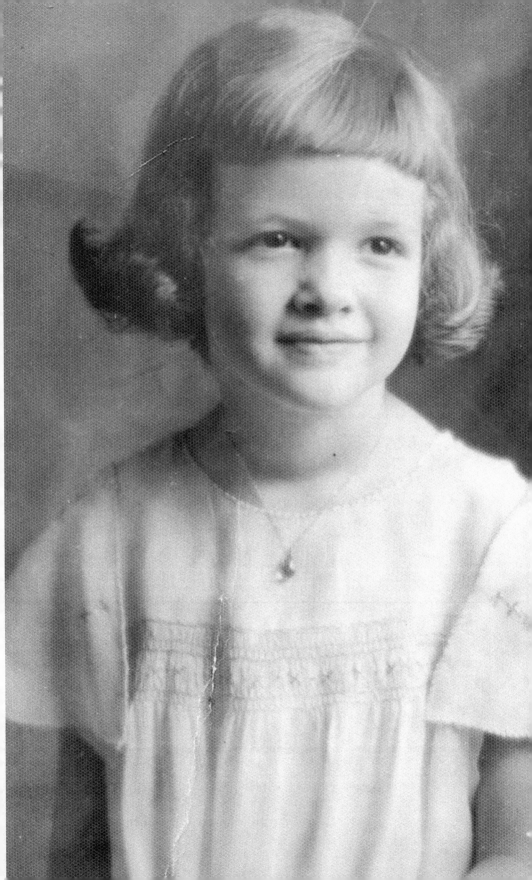

1934 To Billings

I was six, almost seven, and when I looked in the mirror all I could see was a pair of big teeth, with a gap between them. I had outgrown being Daddy Wood's little valentine. My hair was less curly and much darker, in spite of Mother Wood's always rinsing it with lemon juice. I was still skinny, and the hand-me-down clothes were too big for me. I mostly always wore the clothes that came from Mr. Wood's grandchildren, Dolly and Baby, born to his daughter from a previous marriage. For the train trip, Mother Wood seemed to choose the ugliest dress in the box of hand-me-downs. "It won't show dirt. Trains are dirty," she said. It was rust crepe and felt ugly; it smelled like rust.

That year, Edna Wood, who had been trying for several years to persuade Mother that I belonged with "my own people," decided that now was the perfect time for me to join them. I reported to them, on arriving in Billings, Montana in 1934, that Mrs. Wood sent me away from Los Angeles because of the "infantalaralasis." Mother and the twins were there in Billings on a summer visit, having come from Boulder, Colorado. Juneau lived there.

Me, wearing the rust-colored crepe dress for the trip to Billings, 1934

When I was placed in foster care at twenty-one months old, Mrs. Wood had been under the impression that she was to shelter me temporarily, just until Mrs. McKenzie, my errant mother, got back on her feet, or possibly put me up for adoption. The Woods had a twelve-year-old adopted daughter. They had provided a temporary home for several children over the years following the stillbirth of Edna's identical twin boys. She loved little children but didn't want to become too attached to one of them. For a time it was not at all clear to me why the woman who fed me and clothed me was not my mother, and why "That Woman" who "smoked cigarettes and only thought about herself" was my mother.

I was settled on the train with some gifts: a dime-store China doll, a handkerchief, and a compact with my name on it. A woman I had seen several times at the Woods, who seemed always to have a great interest in me and was a welfare worker, came to see me off. She gave me a crumpled dollar bill and said that they would probably have silver dollars in Billings. I put the dollar with a nickel and some pennies in my purse, under the compact and handkerchief. Somewhere in my cardboard suitcase I had another gift, a silver-plated knife, fork, and spoon set, junior-sized, that the Knittles had given me.

The knowledge that I was henceforth going to be able to cut my own meat, with my own knife, made me feel grown up. The knowledge that I would sleep that night in an upper berth, and that I would eat dinner in the dining car, made me secretly, guiltily happy in spite of my sorrow. So as the train hissed and lurched into motion, my fear was tempered by a sense of adventure, until I saw that the first sudden motion had thrown my doll off the seat, breaking her head off quite neatly. My new handkerchief soon became a wet, still crisp ball in my hand.

The rest of the trip is quite vague. I remember a woman inviting me to eat with her in the dining car and encouraging me through the swaying cars and shifting vestibules. I remember eating oatmeal at breakfast and thinking it was very good, perhaps because I had chosen it myself. I remember climbing into the upper berth and then worrying that the porter would forget I was there and might snap it shut like my compact. And I can see the depot in Salt Lake, I very small, the space very large.

In Billings my grown-up sister Juneau, who Mother Wood called "June-e-a," met the train. Juneau was twenty-six years old and called me "Darling." She corrected my pronunciation of her name and smoked a cigarette in the cab. I thought she was just like "That Woman," Mrs. McKenzie. She said that I must remember her, that she had taken me on walks and we had had such fun. I supposed that she had been one of those people in my mother's hotel room, perhaps the one who had burned my arm.

Then I remember the cab stopping in front of a large house, and my mother seeming to float down the walk in a flowing, flowered voile dress. She said, "Megan, darling," and kissed me. When I wiped the spot where she had kissed me, she asked, "You don't like Mother, do you?" and

Juneau and me in Billings, 1934

laughed. We went up several flights of stairs to a hot, dark room, really a suite of rooms: an anteroom, bedroom, and sleeping porch; a space once intended for perhaps two people. As my eyes adjusted to the light, I saw my almost-eighteen-year-old twin sisters, Cynthia and Margery, one sitting on the bed, the other standing by the dresser, both wearing absolutely nothing. My mother said, "Isn't it beastly? It must be a hundred degrees in here." I might as well have walked into Hell; at least I was sure that I would go there for having seen those naked, beautiful, frightening bodies. The only bare body I had ever seen was my own. I didn't know where to look.

I try to recall that first day in Billings. My sisters merge in and out of the darkness, the suffocating heat. I remember Juneau and my mother daubing at their eyes; I thought they were crying because they didn't want me to be there. I don't remember anything about Cynthia, the twin who was sitting on the bed. I remember Mardie, though. She said that I was probably hot in my rust crepe dress. She said that if I wanted to take a nice bath or sponge bath there was a bathroom right down the hall. She said that I probably had a sunsuit in my suitcase. "Do you mind if I look?" she asked, as though she did not have the right to open it without my permission, as though I were a grown up. She said she hoped that I had some sandals because the sidewalks were too hot to go barefooted. But I had never had sandals because Mother Wood thought I needed high-top shoes for my "weak ankles," and because sandals were bad for my feet. "Only less fortunate children wear sandals. Or children whose mothers don't care what happened to their feet," Mother Wood said.

After a cool bath, Mardie combed my hair and tied it with a ribbon. She didn't pull it the way Mother Wood always did, and she told me what nice hair I had. I could not understand what was going on in the room, what they were laughing about, what they were crying about, what they were saying. Mardie must have known or felt my confusion, because she suggested that we go get an ice cream cone.

Outside was so hot the pavement smelled and the asphalt was soft under my shoes. The ice cream cone melted faster than I could eat it and ran down my arms in strawberry and vanilla rivulets. Mardie smiled. "You're going to need another bath by the time we get home."

She called me Meegie and talked about the family in Boulder as though it were my family. She talked about our brother Neil and how handsome he was and how smart. When I referred to my mother as Mrs. McKenzie, she said I should call her Mother, that she loved me very much and that it hurt her when I called her Mrs. McKenzie. She said that there was a beautiful picture of me in Boulder, and that she and Cynthia liked to go into Mother's room just to see it. She said they were very happy to have a baby sister, and that Daddy McKenzie loved me too.

By the end of the walk, I understood that Mother and the twins had come to Billings just for a visit, because Juneau and her husband Harvey Weed were there for his summer engagement playing jazz at the Olde Heidelberg Inn. Mardie and Cynthia would return to Boulder at the end of summer to go to college. I hoped they would take me with them.

Juneau around the time when I first knew her

1934 BILLINGS, A WIDER VIEW

Every female related to Juneau had decided to visit her that summer. Both our mother and her mother-in-law were there; Margery and Cynthia were there, and then I arrived. It couldn't have been a worse time.

Almost as soon as I arrived in Billings, my sisters taught me to question most of what I had accepted to be "everything that was." Wisely, they didn't start their campaign with Jesus himself. In fact, as I recall, they said he was a good man, a very good man. They left it at that.

Someone, probably Mardie, started the "deprogramming" with Sister Aimee. I was quite surprised and angry to learn that none of my three sisters believed as I did that Sister Aimee Semple McPherson, charismatic founder of the Foursquare Church, was a disciple or maybe even an apostle. Mardie claimed that Mrs. McPherson had once disappeared and everyone thought she was dead. She said that when Sister Aimee showed up alive after a few months, she pretended to have been kidnapped, but, according to my sisters, she had just gone off someplace with her boyfriend.

Mrs. Wood had armed me against such heresies. She had warned me that worldly people, people who weren't "born again," made up stories

Drawing that Cynthia did of me in Billings, 1934

My twin sisters, Mardie (left) and Cynthia (right), circa 1934

about Christians. I dismissed what my sisters said—which is not to say that I forgot.

My sisters also told me that the nice man I knew only as Chaunce was my father. Furthermore, Mrs. Maytham, the lady with the long blond hair who had some questionable claim on me, was my grandmother. I was six-and-a-half years old but I had never wondered who my father was; I didn't know I had or needed one. No one had ever mentioned anything at all about a father.

I knew my "real" mother as Mrs. McKenzie and during my short tenure in first grade at Raymond Avenue Grammar School in Los Angeles I was Megan McKenzie; I didn't know that was because when I was born in

Hollywood my mother was married to Mr. Neil B. McKenzie of Boulder, Colorado. I am listed in the 1930 Census as Meegan McKenzie, lodger, two years and six months at 1122 West Seventieth Street in Los Angeles. When I entered second grade at Broadwater Elementary in Billings, I was Megan Brown, because my biological father was Chauncey Rowland Brown. When I returned to my foster home and reenrolled in the Los Angeles public school system, I was Megan Wood, because Edna Wood was afraid someone might take the difference in our names to be a sign that she was a divorcee.

It was a good summer. I learned to ride Juneau's gigantic bicycle, and some days Mardie or Juneau would put me in the basket and pedal down to the public swimming pool. One of Mardie's boyfriends gave me a big box of hexagonal crayons, more colors than I had ever seen—rainbows and rainbows of colors. Everyone said I was very artistic, and someone even put one of my pictures on the wall of the new apartment we moved into. Cynthia and one of her boyfriends took me to a circus, and though I didn't like the show and didn't think the clowns were funny, I loved being there. I liked the tent, much bigger than a revival tent, but I thought overall that revivals were more fun because the music was better.

For a time, I lived with Juneau and Harvey who were renting a small trailer (think more "sheepherder" than "Airstream") in the Kerrs' backyard, friends of Juneau's from some other time. Juneau and Harvey's arrangement with them must have been for room and board. When I arrived, I became one of the boarders at the kitchen table as well as a roomer in the upper bunk of the trailer, sleeping beside its only window.

We often ate with the Kerr family. I remember the meals more for the adventure than the food. In my mind, Mrs. Kerr's father, a very old man, is ever muttering at the kitchen table as he eats with my most prized possession, the child-sized place setting of Lady Hamilton flatware that "Auntie" Gladys and "Uncle" Charlie Knittle had given me as a farewell present when I left California. I loved the Knittles, friends of my foster parents who had wanted to adopt me. When the old man confiscated my silverware, I was outraged. Juneau nudged me, shaking her head, saying that he only wanted to borrow it. I didn't understand why an old man wanted to use my child-sized silver nor did I know why Juneau and Mrs. Kerr humored him. I don't suppose anyone could have explained

Olde Heidelberg Inn, 1940s, Billing Gazette archive

Alzheimer's disease to a six-year-old whose sense of justice didn't extend much beyond herself.

Most afternoons I sat in the Olde Heidelberg Inn, the place where Juneau and Harvey worked, a place I loved. I had never before been somewhere devoted entirely to pleasure, pleasure being largely synonymous with sin. There was dancing—ballroom dancing under a mirror-faceted ball that splattered the dancers with color. There was tap-dancing and acrobatic dancing done by "The Shirley Temple of Montana," a child not much older than I was. I admired her—her Patsy-doll haircut, patent leather tap shoes, white sequined leotard, limber back, and tapping feet—but I knew that I was some other kind of creature entirely and would ever be. So I concluded that she was just a showoff.

Evenings at the Heidelberg were mainly for music, some of which was provided by Harvey, who played piano with the jazz combo. I barely noticed him. When the music blared, my eyes were on the brass, so beautiful in the light: a trumpet, a trombone, sometimes muted with a derby, a saxophone all swinging and swaying to rhythms I had never known. Mother explained that the saxophone was not a true instrument meaning, I suppose, that it was a kind of bastard, half reed and half brass, not fit for the symphony hall, just for jazz.

One week, we watched nightly live performances of a melodrama with a villain, a virtuous woman in need of help, and a hero to rescue her. I learned to sing along with the crowd, "No! No! A thousand times no! I'd rather die than say 'Yes,'" but I didn't really understand what she was refusing to say yes to. I only knew that everyone was having a good time hissing the villain and applauding the hero, so I hissed and clapped right along with them. The hissing was new to me, and much more fun than clapping.

My favorite event at The Old Heidelberg was turtle racing, invented in the twenties, and, according to Wikipedia, still popular at county fairs. In 1934 Billings, it was a gambling game. I have no idea whether the turtles were brought in by the men who bet on them or belonged to some entrepreneur who traveled Montana with his troupe of talented turtles,

Olde Heidelberg Inn postcard

"Betty Boop was not a Christian"

setting up his track wherever there was a gathering of idle men with a little pocket change. The track was a shallow box on the floor, perhaps sixteen by four feet, with sides just high enough to prevent runaways. When I was six, I didn't care a bit about the track, the outcome of the race, or the stomping, shouting cowboys who bet on them. I was only interested in the turtles. Mardie told me they were snapping turtles, just like the ones in Boulder, the ones in the big ditch that ran close to the McKenzie house. (The house I had never seen.) She warned that snapping turtles were dangerous, that her daddy told her, "If one bites you, it won't let go until it thunders." She added that she didn't know whether to believe him or not, because "Daddy liked to tease me sometimes." True or not, the possibility of having a turtle, dear though it might be, as a semipermanent attachment kept me from crowding in too close to the track for a better view. Once a race began, a four-foot-something person was lucky to catch a glimpse of the small colored flags on the backs of the turtles. A time or two, some kind cowboy noticed me and hoisted me onto a wobbling chair from which I could better see them. Before I had actually witnessed a race, I had imagined the turtles to be as frenzied as the crowd, but there they were unhurried and indifferent, content with their own pace and direction.

We also went to forgettable movie matinees fairly often. I only remember two, Shirley Temple in *The Little Colonel* and *Smoky*, by Will James. I don't remember much about *Smoky* actually, but I remember being shocked by the "Boop-Oop-a-Doop" cartoon that preceded it. Betty Boop was *not* a Christian. Later, Juneau took me to Will James's ranch. I don't remember him, a friend of Juneau's from her Hollywood days, but I will never forget that while we were there Juneau called my attention to the song of a meadowlark.

My sisters weren't my only tutors in Billings. Some of my most valuable lessons were self-taught. I learned that just being out of sight was not enough to keep evildoers from the consequences of their acts. If one can hear voices in the kitchen below, it is unwise to pee on the lath floor of the attic, no matter how convenient it may be. Next, I learned that to be successful at anything, even lying, one needs to know a little something. That is, to succeed even at hooky, one needs to know the school schedule and to be aware of the absolute tyranny of the clock.

Specifically, not long after I entered second grade at Broadwater Elementary School, our class, or perhaps the entire school, was given a "quarter holiday" and dismissed early. A few days later I realized that I would rather not be in school all afternoon. What was to keep me from taking another quarter holiday for myself? Who would guess that the other children were still in school? I took off for the Kerr's house.

To my surprise, Juneau guessed. She met me at the door, "What are you doing home?" When I said it was a quarter holiday, she didn't raise her voice or call me a liar. She just explained that quarter holidays never start in the middle of the day and said something like, "If they began at noon, they would be called '*half* holidays.' I think we'd better get you back to school." A few days after that, Juneau bought me a Mickey Mouse watch made by Ingersoll. According to my internet research, that watch cost three dollars in 1934. The standard wage then was twenty-five cents an hour, meaning that Juneau had to wait tables for a day and a half at the Olde Heidelberg to pay for it.

Money was very tight, in general, and another vivid memory from school in Billings was wearing a new dress that my mother had eked out of an old beige challis dress of her own. My dress had long sleeves and it buttoned down the front. I loved it. It made me feel grown up, loved. I felt something like pride, before I heard the teacher say. "Megan, go take off your coat."

One day, as a reward to the class for perfect attendance, we were all herded upstairs to the third floor where we got to slide down the fire escape. Broadwater School had a wonderful fire escape, an enclosed spiral slide. The other kids were jubilant. I listened to their squeals and laughter wishing I could join the fun. I wanted to be one of them. But I was not. I was afraid, and I was ashamed.

I was most comfortable at home. Juneau told me stories that made me laugh or helped me see. Nice stories that I could step into. I wonder if my eldest sister knew what she was doing, if she knew that she had planted seeds that could, over time, crack granite. She read me Rudyard Kipling's *Just So Stories*: "How the Rhinoceros Got His Skin," "How the Camel Got His Hump," "How the Elephant Got His Trunk." These beasts were animated. They changed, improved themselves. Kipling's style was livelier than Moses's. "The great grey-green, greasy Limpopo River" was also a river of words, fun to hear. The River Jordan was just water. I wonder now if Moses wasn't a little too caught up in all that begetting to pay attention to the small details that might have made Genesis a better read.

Juneau was a wonderful teacher; she never belabored the point of a story, but she helped me experience it for myself. I understood how foolish the emperor was to believe he was wearing clothes that he himself couldn't see. I felt acutely embarrassed imagining myself parading down the street with no clothes on. As with the Bible stories I had heard, I didn't think about what it meant; I just digested it. I absolutely loved "reading."

I imagined everyone was as delighted as I with the arrangement that lasted well into the school year. Lasted until a northern wind ruffled the window and piped through its surrounding cracks. Lasted until a California child, a stranger to winter, could warm her heart by stomping on the ice that covered the puddles in the yard. Of course, the child, who could never get warm enough no matter how tightly her blankets were tucked, was never aware of the restless couple in the lower bunk, ever aware of her hovering above.

Broadwater Elementary in its early days

1935 Billings Turns Cold

In early fall the twins had left for college. I didn't care about losing Cynthia, who was pretty and aloof and who sometimes said things that made me feel that I was not really one of the family, that I was not one of them. But Mardie's departure was devastating. I had always hoped that when the time came she would want to take me with her. My main interest in school that fall was learning enough to write to her, with the hope of convincing her that she would really be much happier attending the Normal School in Billings than she could ever be at the University of Colorado in Boulder.

It had become very cold and I had seen my first snow and discovered that it could numb one's feet, and that when it melted it turned to slush, all unexpected by a California child. It was a little like discovering that a darling little dog will snap at you. I missed feeling warm. I missed Mardie. I don't remember school.

I remember Mother and Juneau wrapping presents in colored cellophane, not for the family, but for a store "to get a little extra money." And we had a Christmas tree with real candles; we strung cranberries for its only decorations. I loved the candlelit tree because it was so beautiful

Mr. McKenzie, "Daddy Neil" to Juneau, circa 1932

Toy baby grand piano like the one given to me for Christmas in 1934

and the candles were so dangerous. I was ever mindful of the stories of blazing Christmas trees and incinerated houses filled with Christmas presents and children. I remember Juneau teaching me how to draw a five-pointed star, but I think she made the one that topped the tree.

Christmas Day, my gift was a toy baby grand piano with stenciled black keys. It was a little narrower than the laptop computer I am writing on. I learned to play "Auld Lang Syne," and was only slightly bothered that I had no idea at all what the words meant.

On January 5, Mother wrote in her diary, "no mail.... Colder today.... Megan is sweet. I love her." The rest of the yearbook is blank. Because January 5 was the day that the doorbell rang.

I remember Mother lying on the couch with a small piece of paper clutched in her hand. I can still see her as though in a photograph: She is wearing a maroon skirt that buttoned all the way down the side. She is looking away from me as she tells me that she has to leave.

I didn't know why she was crying; I didn't know why I wanted to comfort her. She had to go back to Boulder because someone was very sick. A day or two later, Juneau told me that "Daddy Neil," had died of pneumonia and that Mother got there too late to say goodbye.

* * *

In January of '35, Juneau was still working at the Olde Heidelberg but Harvey no longer had a steady job. The post-prohibition bar boom had slowed to the point that tavern owners hoped a little music might help pick up business, so he was picking up the occasional night. But there were plenty of out-of-work piano players who'd be glad to make a buck or two for a couple of hours. The bartender might even throw in a few drinks. No more gigs like the Olde Heidelberg though.

When Juneau met my train in Billings, she was a worldly woman. She had already lived through the highs of Hollywood in the 1920s and the lows of the 1930s. Before that, she had witnessed the fall from grace of the McKenzie family as a whole and of her mother in particular. She must had have heard the rumors that her father, Dr. Eikner, had killed somebody "in cold blood," but that he was justified because her mother was a tramp.

As I try to understand what happened to her life, I wonder how long it took Juneau herself to understand what went wrong with Harvey. When did she know he was in terrible trouble? Was she burdened with that knowledge all that year, just trying to get through each day? Even though I lived with Harvey and Juneau in close quarters for most of my year in Billings, I didn't know him at all. I don't remember ever even talking with him, although it must have happened every day. I suppose most of us forget the routine things as soon as they become routine. They become the background of our lives, the fabric, but I barely remember him. He had sharp features that I didn't find pleasing. I think I was just more accustomed to the four female faces I saw regularly during the summer of 1934. When the twins returned to Boulder at the end of summer, there were just two faces, Mother's and Juneau's, but Mother's was not a constant. I don't remember her much before the Christmas season. Then she was gone, and I was just with Juneau and Harvey.

Harvey and Juneau sometime after leaving Billings

After Mother left, the three of us moved several times. As usual, I only remember fragments. I remember the day Juneau climbed the steep flight of stairs hugging a bag of groceries. She was smiling. She had won five dollars in the Chinese lottery. Even before she put the groceries away, she made us tea. I think my "tea" was just hot water, milk, and sugar. But I can still remember how good it was, how sweet the celebration.

The next scene is of those same stairs, but from a different angle. I can't actually see the stairs themselves, but I know they are there behind the dirty white door at the bottom, the exit that opens onto a small concrete square, not much wider than the door itself. The door isn't just closed; it's locked. There's a piece of paper on it. Juneau's steamer trunk is standing on end on the concrete. When Juneau comes home, she yanks the paper off the door and I learn a new word. EVICTED.

After that, we lived in a room on the south side of Billings, past the tracks, that was too small for the steamer trunk. I remember that place well. I can almost smell it. There wasn't much else to remember. It was a bare room with a dresser and one double bed. I slept there nights with Juneau, and Harvey slept during the day. The bathroom was down the hall. With such a high demand for tub space, bathing was a problem. Juneau and I bathed together, or sometimes she would just ask me to save my bathwater.

During that time, Harvey played piano in a Chinese bar on the South Side. He would sleep all day and work or drink or both, all night. I rarely saw him. Even as a child I knew that the South Side was not a choice area of town. I remember going to an opium den there, too, but the memory is so vague that now I wonder if it is one of those "implanted memories" maybe put in my head by Mrs. Wood's questions about what I did while I was in Billings, while in a Chinese bar. I just can't quite remember what it is that I remember about it. Were there men on cots? Curtains? Beads? Smoke? I do know, from looking it up recently, that there were such places in that very neighborhood, but I cannot imagine why or how I could have come to be in one of them, even for a minute.

The last place we lived, we again shared the same bed, though not at the same time, in a small upstairs room in what I now suppose was a rooming house. Harvey still worked most of the night and slept much of the day. When he didn't work, he didn't hang around.

One day Harvey came home midmorning from what Juneau told me was a walk in the park. He was tearing at himself and screaming, "They're all over me! Get them off of me! Get them off of me!" When Juneau asked him what "they" were, he cried, "Ticks! Can't you see?"

A few days after Harvey had come in from his tortured "walk in the park," in late June it might have been, Juneau put me on a bus bound for Butte, Montana. I was to meet the Kelly family, work friends of Mr. Wood. They just happened to be visiting relatives in Butte at the very time Mrs. Wood received a frantic telegram from either Juneau or Mother. I was going back to Los Angeles. Mr. Kelly had offered me a ride in the back seat, along with his daughter Eileen. I can remember Eileen's face and figure far better than I can remember Harvey's. She was chubby. Her dress was actually tight on her little barrel-shaped body. Her face was round and she had short blond hair that had been waved. I was tall and gangly. We must have been a funny pair. Mrs. Wood had sent me some clothes in care of the Kellys: green overalls and a yellow shirt made of a rough, muslin-like fabric with tiny brown flecks in it. I loved the clothes even though they were too big. There's a picture of me, standing on a slope in the Kelly's back yard, taken with a Brownie camera.

Although I was happy to return to what I still thought of as home, I know I cried a little when Juneau put me on the bus to Butte. Even though it was abrupt, it didn't seem related to a precipitating event. It didn't seem like I was being banished. I'm not sure what I thought and can't remember at all what I felt. I'm not sure that I had any expectation at all of continuity, or cause and effect. Things just happened. Later, I tried to string them together.

Irene Kelly and her dad in Butte, Montana, July 1935

Coda

I never saw Juneau again. She sent me books for a while. *A Child's Garden of Verses*, *Ferdinand*, and *Water Babies* are among the ones I remember. I read those some, thumbed idly through others, reread my favorites, and placed all of them on one of the two lower shelves in the small bookcase in the dining room. The four upper shelves were taken up by Mrs. Wood's collection of small china dogs and other such treasures. Every Saturday, the day I was assigned to dust the knick-knack shelves, I thought of Juneau. I don't think I wondered about her. I put her in a familiar place and just left her there, sitting in the doorway of the trailer, reading *The Just So Stories* to me or coming up the stairs with a big bag of groceries and a smile. I don't remember having any news of her. No one mentioned that she and Harvey had moved to the east coast, or that Harvey had been in a sanitarium in Stamford, Connecticut, for over two years.

It wasn't until the fall of 1938, when Mrs. Wood handed me a small newspaper clipping that said Juneau Eikner Weed had been found dead on a Long Island beach, that I knew anything at all about what had happened to Juneau after she put me on the bus to Butte. Nor can I remember how my eleven-year-old self felt when I read that the sister who had told me the story of the emperor's new clothes, who had taught me to read by reading *When We Were Very Young* with me (without my suspecting that she was making up for the school I had missed), who had taught me to listen to the song of a meadow lark, who had made wonderful sandwiches from nothing but a slice of sweet white onion between two slices of white bread, who had taught me to be aware of life itself, had been murdered.

Photo of Juneau that the newspapers used in reporting her death

1935 BACK TO CALIFORNIA

I remember nothing of the trip back to California beyond the brief stay in Butte, Montana, where the Kelly family met me. It seemed sudden but it must have been planned a bit ahead, through an interchange of special delivery letters or an exchange of telegrams. Long distance calling would have been far too expensive for either the Woods or Juneau; furthermore, it would have been the strangest of coincidences for the Kelly family to be in Butte at the very time I was to arrive.

When I had left Los Angeles in 1934, I was leaving home. I heard Miss Logan, the case worker, tell Mrs. Wood that I could not come back. In a sense, she was right, because a year later, when I returned to the same house on West Seventieth Street, it was no longer my home. It was my foster home. I was not a part of the family. I had become a Brown, and my newly acquired name was especially unwelcome. Concerned that a Megan Brown might give people the impression that she was divorced, she enrolled me as Megan Wood.

I suppose everything we are exposed to changes us in ways that we are not fully aware of at the time. As a seven-year-old, I was completely unaware that my year in Billings had already changed me in fundamental

Me, in Butte, Montana, 1935

ways. I had lost, forever, the ability to be certain, to believe fully in anything at all. I had become incapable of the blind faith I had once had. I was not quite a doubter; I was a questioner.

My exposure to the world of the worldly was enormously instructive. It turns out that I had been among my own people. I'm not sure that I was ever again as cozy as I had been before going to Billings. I could not un-know any of what I had seen. Even though at the time I had very little, if any, understanding of the importance of that year, that I was no longer either completely malleable or capable of certitude. There was another way to look at everything in the world. There were choices. I had questions.

From my foster mother's perspective, I probably seemed less cooperative. I wanted to stay up later and get up earlier. I wanted a regular bicycle, not one that I could only ride on the sidewalk. I wanted hot lunches instead of a new lunch pail. I wanted to wear my hair the way I had in Billings. (I began to hear words like incorrigible.) As I remember it, those concerns were minor. The first significant problem for me arose in church.

The Sunday that Sister Annabelle, my foster mother's friend, asked me if I would like to be saved, my backside was hurting and I must have said, "I guess so," or something like that because she grabbed my arm and kind of shoved me out to the aisle and down toward the altar, where all the other sinners were down on their knees crying and praying to Jesus. There was just enough room for me to squeeze in and kneel. Sister Annabelle, a heavy woman (I once heard Mr. Wood describe her as a glutton), was right behind me, rocking back and forth and gradually mashing me into the altar with each forward lunge as she plead with The Lord to save my soul. Soon, my bony knees hurt so that, to save me, I could not focus on my soul. As I attempted to escape being crushed, Miss Annabelle burst into tears and a spate of "thank-yous" and "praise the Lords."

The Foursquare Church taught through repetition that "my sins rose as high as a mountain," but I also did feel that I had committed an unforgivable sin by not saying that Mrs. Wood's friend, Sister Annabelle, was mistaken when she announced that I had been "saved." I could have told the truth right then and there. I could have said, "No. I just got tired of praying for forgiveness, and my knees hurt from kneeling." I could have said that Sister Annabelle mistook my getting up for redemption. I said nothing at all.

At first, I wasn't absolutely sure. I mean that I didn't feel like any better of a person when I got off my knees than I had before Sister Annabelle led me to the altar and motioned for me to kneel, but I thought maybe that was what salvation felt like. So I decided to wait and see what happened. When I knelt beside my bed that night, I asked Jesus for a sign.

The next day at school, nothing happened. I wasn't a bit different. I still didn't straighten out the mess in my desk. I still couldn't choke down the dry cheese sandwich Mrs. Wood wrapped in wax paper and put in my lunch box. I tried. I took a few bites before I threw it in the trash along with the wadded wax paper and the apple core. I still hated the way the thermos bottle smelled when I poured the milk into the aluminum cup, so I poured what was left in the bottle into the gravel under the bench I was sitting on. That was wasteful, but it was better than gagging, even if it meant that some little child in China would have to go without milk.

I think I might even have farted that very afternoon or maybe it was another afternoon; anyway, when the boys started pointing at each other, I just kept practicing my penmanship, which was pretty much the same thing as lying. It was worse than that: Even if it wasn't on purpose, it was a terrible thing to do and I was letting someone else take the blame for it. Even when Miss Ashe opened a window and said it was stuffy, I just kept doing my penmanship.

I still had that same old pile of sins. I was certain that Mrs. Wood suspected or maybe even knew that I was a hypocrite and a liar.

1935 Skipping Ahead

I must have learned a good bit of what I was sent to learn at Broadwater Elementary School in Billings, though I don't recall a single thing about the process. When I returned to Raymond Avenue in Los Angeles, shortly after starting I was put ahead a semester.

I believe my sisters taught me to read during the summer before I had enrolled in school in Billings. I know that it was Juneau who taught me to want to read. She walked me through *A Child's Garden of Verses*, where I learned to watch shadows. She taught me to bob down "the great grey-green, greasy Limpopo," and to feel the crumbs beneath the skin of a rhinoceros. She and Rudyard Kipling and Robert Louis Stevenson did far more than that, however; they taught me new ways to look and listen to things. They taught me to have fun.

I don't know how I learned the times tables or the art of carrying and borrowing but those were the skills that put me a little bit ahead by shortening third grade to a single semester. Among the memories preserved from Miss Ashe's third-grade class is the day I learned that the sun did not emerge from the earth to float overhead all day before gradually settling back into the ground or the ocean (depending, I supposed, on

A portrait taken after my return from Billings

whichever was beneath it at the time), although I was not entirely convinced otherwise by Miss Ashe's demonstration. She placed a big, red, white, and green, inflatable beach ball atop a stool beside her desk.

She told us the ball was the sun and that even though the sun looked smaller than the earth it was actually much bigger. It just appeared to be small because it was so far away. Then she held a ping-pong ball in her hand and moved it in a half orbit (obstructed by her desk) between the rubber sun and her pupils, saying "This is the earth. It goes all the way around the sun every year. Just imagine!" (I know I was imagining getting my hands on the beautiful beach ball.) "And all of the time that it is traveling around the sun, the world is spinning like a top." Miss Ashe pirouetted.

Her words, rather than her performance, raised some serious and abiding questions in my mind about the difference between what things seem to be and what they turn out to be. Of course, on that day, I had no inkling of how thoroughly Miss Ashe had shaken up my world. Neither of us suspected that the underlying lesson was in relativity and the improbability of one's ever really knowing anything for sure.

Another day, Miss Ashe showed the class how to use a ruler. Peter Larsen, a restless little blond boy, who seemed to know the answer to everything before Miss Ashe had even asked the question, had done some awful thing—like picking his nose or whispering behind his hand, or poking the kid in front of him. The teacher called him to the front of the room and, clenching a ruler, she ordered him to put his hands flat on her desk. She had whacked an offending hand just once before Peter dashed from the room. Miss Ashe ran after him. Allegedly, she chased him out of the building and off the school grounds. The next day, the prevailing whisper was that she had pursued him all the way home. This is the story, true or not, that I have carried around in my head for nearly eighty years.

I suppose that spontaneous demonstration of rules and rulers stuck with me because I understood and admired the unruly kid far more than I either understood or admired Miss Ashe. And because I never really believed that Miss Ashe caught up with him.

One day, Miss Ashe asked the class to tell her what our fathers did for a living. I don't know what her purpose was. Perhaps the question was part of a survey of the school population, but it could have been the

Me, age eight, on swing with Eleanor, Mr. Woods' granddaughter, and Sue Mae

beginning of a social studies unit about families. When I said that my father was a director, she said, "A movie director?" and asked me what his name was. I said it was "Chaunce." She asked me to repeat it, scowled, and told me to write his name on the blackboard. I scrawled Ch before I stopped to wonder au? aw? ough? augh? I had no idea how to spell it. Unfortunately, because I had learned only the year before that Chaunce was my father, I was missing certain critical information: I was not sure what a father was or how one qualified for the title. I had no idea what a director did or was, and I had no clue what his last name was. I didn't know that someone called Rowland C. Brown was Chauncey Rowland Brown who was the man my mother called Chaunce, but who was generally known as Rowland. I was just feeling rather wonderful because I had a father and knew it.

When Miss Ashe told me to sit down. I could feel everyone in the room staring at me and saying to themselves "She's stupid and she is a liar. I hate her."

* * *

Sometimes it seems to me that I remember every moment I spent at Raymond Avenue Grammar School, from the first discordant bell to the final one. I wonder now why those terrible jangling noises that sawed our days off from our lives were called "bells." But I remember waiting, tailbone aching, for the bell that allowed us to leave.

I remember the teachers not for what they taught but for their evil tempers, their genius for humiliating students. In grade school the teachers were all women, most of whom had probably not chosen teaching as a career but as an escape hatch in case their lives, their love affairs, soured.

I remember only one exception, one in five years of grade school, a woman who the other teachers addressed as "Doctor," and who seemed to know something of the mystery of things. She brought in outsiders to show us things like the magic of chemistry. For instance, one could change ordinary, colorless tap water to red or blue just by pouring into it drops of something else that looked just like the plain water. She and the visitors taught us to wonder and to hear and think. She knew more than rules.

I can see the third-grade teacher throwing chairs, the small wooden chairs which we sat in during reading—throwing them in every direction. Another woman, with a mouth that had been drawn by ruler, smashed a little girl's watch as a lesson, I suppose in courtesy. "It is not polite to look at your watch when I am talking to you." That was the same teacher who asked me to write my father's name on the blackboard. .

Another, a sweet-faced teacher, the one everyone hoped to get for sixth grade, shamed Naomi Pearl, a beautiful little girl with curly hair, a girl who was often the first student to have the right answer. We were playing a game invented by the teacher in which students ticketed their classmates for grammatical errors in oral reports. Naomi and I had both detected an error in the speaker's presentation but she began to claim the ticket slightly ahead of me, "Give me a—." Before Naomi could say "ticket," the teacher hissed, "That's the trouble with you Jews. Gimme, gimme, gimme." Her mouth puckered around the word "Jews."

Naomi responded, very quietly, "Sometimes I don't think you Christians are very nice either," picked up her books, and walked out of the room. I wish I could now report that I had a social conscience, that I got up and walked out too. I didn't. I didn't really understand the incident. I only knew what my experience allowed me to know. Disgrace. And I knew that part of the disgrace was my own.

The boy who sat behind me in fourth grade once poked me on the shoulder, and slid a tiny scrap of paper toward me, which I was supposed to accept without attracting anyone's attention. The message was straightforward. "I love you." Immediately, without hesitation, I was in love with him. All day long I was in love. The next morning I raced to school, eager to see him, perhaps even to touch him. When I approached him, standing with his friends, he said, "Chinaman," and his friends laughed.

I have no idea what impulse caused him to say that particular word. Perhaps he was trying to give a name to my strangeness, my difference from the others. His friends must have enjoyed the impact of the word on me, however, because for the next five years I was taunted with "Chink-a-chink-a Chinaman," or "Chink." It was not a nickname, but a label, like "Nigger" or "Kike." I wonder if that was the origin of my discomfort with labels of any type, unless they are firmly attached to cans, bottles, and boxes, whose contents can be expected to fulfill, in every respect, the promise of the label.

One thing I know now is that teaching is an act of love—and so is learning.

1940 GAMINE

Finally, I was adolescent. Though if "adolescence" means growing into adulthood I feel that I never fully emerged from that stage, that I am only now approaching the full richness and wisdom of maturity, of final ripeness. Someone should pluck me soon.

The first sign was a pimple on my nose. Karen Knudsen pointed it out; Mother Wood could probably not see it. I think that my menarche must have exactly coincided with Mother Wood's menopause, because at just that time she began complaining of hot flashes and dizzy spells, of rheumatism and headaches. She searched for a healer, beginning with the minister of her church and ending with a Chinese herbalist. She said it was her religion that forbade her to seek help from a bona fide physician. She believed that herbs were preferable to regular medicine because God made them. They looked ungodly, though, and the daily brewing of roots, barks, lichens, and sticks filled the house with unfamiliar odors. She grimaced as she drank the tea, which was sometimes muddy black, sometimes clear amber.

I wonder now about her. Was she simply hoping for the return of youth? She always seemed so old. Was she so hungry for a touch of mystery or of the exotic that she would have been willing to drink silt from

Me, having an ice cream cone on a trip to San Francisco, 1935. I don't have any photos between 1936 and 1942.

Crestline cabin that is similar to the "Dew Drop Inn"

the Yangtze River? Is it possible, as my son Michael has suggested, that the primary ingredient in the concoction was cannabis? Was the ritual of preparing her own medicine, of steeping the whole household in its vapors, a way of sharing her infirmity?

That year, in the middle of our two-week vacation in the mountains, I began to menstruate. We were staying in a rented mountain cabin in Crestline and Mrs. Wood decided I was finally old enough to go horseback riding. I was thrilled. The ride did not include instruction of any sort, so I just hung on to the horn of the western saddle and bounced around like a rag doll. By the time I got back to the cabin, my underpants felt sticky.

When I got back to our cabin, the "Dew Drop Inn," I was shocked to find them spotted with blood and I was too embarrassed to tell Mrs. Wood and hid them in a bathroom drawer. Mother Wood had given me a pamphlet from a Kotex box, sometime after the eruption of the pimple. And DeLoris had once shown me a bloody Kotex. But I had no idea what menstruation was, only that it happened, and that it was referred to as "coming sick." So when it began, I was mortified. It was such a filthy thing, so shameful; I didn't want anyone to know.

I did manage to tell DeLoris my terrible secret, which she promptly relayed to Mrs. Wood, who was even more upset than I had imagined she would be. She scolded, vilified, and cried, then grew sentimental. "Why? Why did you start here?" That led to, "I've bought you a little belt with some little gold safety pins...everything. A pretty little pink belt...but it's all at home." Not only did I feel dirty, I felt responsible for destroying her dream, for rejecting her thoughtful gift. Pure shame.

I did not like the nasty issue of my body. I hated the walnut-sized breasts, which had erupted like the pimple, perhaps at the same moment. I knew of course that women had tits, and that younger children, male and female, snickered when older girls bounced by, but I was not a woman; I was a gawky, thirteen-year-old girl, who would have liked very much to be a gawky, breast-free, thirteen-year-old boy. Once, my foster sister had told me that sometimes, when girls are twelve or thirteen, they change into boys. I had thought I might be like that. But it didn't happen.

Still, I don't know whether it was my developing body or my developing mind that caused my general discontent. Mother Wood complained that I did nothing, absolutely nothing, but stare into space. (When Michael was thirteen his seventh-grade teacher complained, "He just stares out the window, like someone with something on his mind." That must be the real fear, that the powerless, the docile, might begin to think, in spite of the school's best efforts, the church's, and the parents'.) I'm not at all sure that I was thinking, though I probably had a small snarl of thoughts I was trying to untangle. I didn't read much that troubled my mind. I read and reread *A Tale of Two Cities*, *Ramona*, and *Riders of the Purple Sage*. I read *Popular Mechanics* and imagined making things that worked out of things that did nothing at all. But I didn't make anything, because I had no tools, and because I would not have been able to build and use the things that I most wanted to. I wanted to build a beautiful car out of orange crates, one that would roll on forever.

I started to ninth grade the January after Pearl Harbor, and whether my spirits had been lifted by the excitement of impending disaster or the joy of being an American whose own country was in the process of saving the world, I couldn't say, but I suddenly felt a part of things, a member. I wrote patriotic poems that were published by the public school magazine, a citywide anthology. Writing the poems brought tears to my eyes. I got good grades and had friends. I was no longer "Chinaman," perhaps because nobody was. Now the Chinese were our very best friends, brave and courageous.

There were balloons around Los Angeles the last year that I was there, fat, lumpish, gray things on cables—barrage balloons surrounding the factories. They were supposed to deter enemy aircraft or reassure the workers. They were amusing. It was an exciting time. We had just become involved in the war, and suddenly sailors were respectable and diligent. But Japanese truck farmers were trying to poison us, were sending messages from their trucks. Their children, who had excelled in school, who had once been as harmless and charming as dolls, were now "Japs" and cowards.

Barrage Balloons like these surrounded factories, Thomas & Katherine Detre Library & Archives

An old Japanese woman was said to have hanged herself in the Los Angeles County Jail. She had Japanese War Bonds pinned to her petticoat, the papers said.

Mother Wood was an air-raid warden who kept a full stirrup pump and a bucket of sand ever ready by the back gate. She was issued a World War I helmet and gas mask. We had a chart in the bathroom by which we could identify any poisonous gas by smell or the type of lesion it created.

My home life was very restrictive during this time. One Saturday, Mother Wood allowed me to go to the movies with my friends, the first time I had ever gone without her. With her permission I rode the bus with my friends toward downtown, a rare adventure of camaraderie. We saw an innocuous musical comedy but it was so much fun for me. The next week, they phoned to invite me to join them at the movies again but this time Mother Wood informed them I would not be allowed to go again, to my anger and embarrassment. It turned out she was very upset to have not been included in the invitation.

I began to question all of the values of my foster home. I began to doubt that Mother Wood was even saved. I began to suspect that no one was, that it was the same for her as it had been for me: she would prefer eternal damnation to public admission of her own hypocrisy. I asked for some sign, some small thing by which I might understand the power of God, the caring. I prayed that He would cause the minister's son to fall in love with me. I prayed that He would heal Mother Wood, take away her migraines, her rheumatism, her hot flashes, her whine.

I found it increasingly difficult to understand either the fairness or the wisdom of a god who made himself known to so few, who revealed himself through such instruments as the shrewish blue-haired woman in our church who would suddenly jump to her feet, throw her head back, and speak in tongues. I puzzled over the fact that our minister's small daughter had been crushed by a car, perhaps on the same day that some bag of flesh had tottered forward to be healed by the simple laying on of the hands.

The last year I was at the Woods, scarcely a week passed that I did not hear the threat that had once made me cower: "You straighten up right now or I'll send you to live with your own people. Let them deal with you."

One time I said, "Good. Do it, goddammit."

1941 BELONGING IN WAR

When World War II finally came to us everything changed. I was fourteen. I feared war above all human ills. It was so all-embracing, so random. Of course, the war had been going on for over two years before Pearl Harbor. Long before the invasion of Poland I had heard preachers describe terrible wars of the past and prophesy those yet to come. I had learned that the harm done by war outlasts the war itself. On the corner of Florence and Vermont, I had seen a legless man whose torso perched on a little wooden platform with skate wheels or maybe casters. He sold pencils. Mother Wood said, "He lost his legs in the World War."

On one Sunday drive, Mr. Wood pointed out a white building set back from the highway. "That's Sawtelle," he said, adding that it was full of soldiers who had been gassed twenty years before in the World War. Mustard gas. After the war in Europe started, I used to wake in the middle of the night with my heart pounding from dreams of a sky blackened with planes like a plague of locusts. "War and rumors of wars" heralded the Apocalypse, the Second Coming, and the Judgment Day. My incipient agnosticism allowed plenty of room to fear such possibilities. I didn't yet know enough to simply not know. I was just a skeptic. I doubted nearly

Sawtelle Veteran's Home, Los Angeles, circa 1900, Photo: California Historical Society Digital object ID: CHS2013.1297

everything: Christian doctrine, the wisdom of my teachers, and my own reasoning. The one person I believed in was the only president I had ever known, Franklin Delano Roosevelt, and the one thing I believed in was America. I still do, though not in the same way at all. I believe in the opportunity we still have to become far better than we are.

The shock of Pearl Harbor was not that we had been plunged into war. Every school kid was aware of the fighting in Europe. Huge headlines proclaimed the failure of France's Maginot Line and the heroism of the British people in their small boats at Dunkirk. I must not have been the only adolescent American who felt a little ashamed of being left out of something that we should have been involved in. California grade schools stressed Asian and Latin American history over both American and European history. Before Pearl Harbor, when I was learning about China and Japan in the third and fourth grade, I had been taught that Japanese schoolbooks were nothing like Dick and Jane. Miss Ashe, my fourth-grade teacher, who had visited Japan the summer before, told us that their primers had pictures of soldiers in them. Little Japanese boys were learning to be soldiers, to die for an emperor they believed to be a descendant of the sun. That same teacher told us that Japanese people were not innovative like Americans. They didn't invent things like telephones and electric lights and Victrolas. They were very good at borrowing other people's ideas and changing them. She said to remember the three A's: adopt, adapt, adept.

Everything I had learned about the Japanese made them the most different of all people from Americans, the most foreign. They kept to themselves. Sachiko, the very quiet, very smart little girl in my fourth-grade class, who sat in the front row next to the window every day of the week, went to Japanese school on Saturdays. That was even stranger than going to Sunday School on Saturday.

The Japanese people in the vegetable market on Vermont Avenue, where Mother Wood sent me to do the daily shopping for a head of lettuce or a bunch of carrots, didn't speak English. They wrapped the lettuce in a page from a Japanese newspaper. The "Japs" were the people who made all those cheap mechanical toys out of tin cans. "Made in Japan" meant "not very good." My dime-store china doll whose head broke off before the train rolled out of Los Angeles on its way to Billings wasn't Chinese at all. It was made in Japan.

Mother Wood had never trusted "Japs." They were sneaky. They had little slanty eyes that meant they had something to hide. They didn't cook fish before they ate it. They just caught it and ate it. It made Mother Wood and me sick to think of eating a fish raw.

* * *

I knew far less about the damning characteristics of Germans. The Schultzes down the street were a little hard to understand because they spoke with an accent, but they spoke English and they looked almost like Americans. The Knittle family had come from Germany. They were the nicest people I knew. They even wanted to adopt me, but my mother said no. Gladys Knittle was Mother Wood's best friend. She was a German Jew, but that was all right, because she was also a Christian Jew. She and Uncle Charlie Knittle weren't Nazis, they were Nazarenes. Uncle Charlie Knittle was an artist. He thought I was an artist too. Uncle Charlie's brother, Uncle Louis, made little wooden windmills to put in front yards, and his wife, Auntie Gertie, made thick noodles. They let me look through their stereoscope when I visited. Germans were nice. But I had more than first-hand knowledge of the German nature. I had also learned in junior high school that the three B's, Brahms, Beethoven, and Bach, had written nearly all classical music. (I can now see how skilled my teachers were at supplying mnemonics for remembering stereotypes.)

All I knew when the war began in 1939 was that "Nazi" sounded a lot like "nasty" and that Hitler was a funny little man with a mustache. I knew he was planning to take over Europe, but the Maginot Line would stop him. He couldn't possibly get past.

But then I learned something else about Germany and the Third Reich, at Christmas dinner at the Knittles. We always went to their house on Christmas. That day they had another guest, a woman who had just arrived in the United States from Europe. She was very emotional, tearful at times. She had a rather heavy accent, so I didn't understand all that she was saying. She reported that something terrible was going on. She said that German children were being turned against their parents and organized. Taken away. Taught hate. "Youth movement.... Huge rally.... Thousands.... Just boys.... Marching... Swastikas everywhere.... Jews...not allowed business...swastikas... smashed windows.... Jewish children...not allowed in school...whole families disappearing overnight...deported...."

I think most Americans have come to think of the evacuation of Japanese Americans as being similar to the treatment of Jews by the Nazis. Perhaps because I lived in California and was exposed not only to the propaganda and overemphasis of newspaper headlines but the reality of virtually all of the fruit and vegetables that I had ever eaten having been grown by Japanese people, wrapped in Japanese language newspapers, and sold in the neighborhood grocery store by people who spoke just enough English to make change, I don't completely share a politically correct view of the relocation camps. Los Angeles Harbor was surrounded by people of Japanese ancestry, two thirds of whom were American citizens. The other third were denied the possibility of citizenship because they were Asians who had not been born in America. Yes, there can be no doubt of the role of racism in the evacuation from the West Coast of over a hundred thousand people but the official justification for it seemed rational to me at the time.

We were told that some of the Japanese Americans might have greater loyalty to their ancestral land than to a country that had rarely been a welcoming host. Later I heard that there was also the prevalent rumor that it was for their own protection, largely because of the persistent threat of harm to all Californians of Asian ancestry by other Californians.

I wish I could say that I knew at the time that the evacuation was wrong, so unjust, but when I was fourteen, I didn't question its necessity. I might have had some questions, but necessity usually trumps justice. From this distance in both time and space, the evacuation appears to have been apparently unnecessary. But now is not then.

My own feelings on December 7, 1941, were much the same as those I felt on 9/11. In both instances I was incredulous. I just couldn't believe what had happened nor could I understand why it had. Why would Japan attack us? Then I had a "Why me?" reaction. What had we ever done to them? My confusion quickly turned to rage.

The reaction of the people in Los Angeles was about the same as that of New Yorkers on 9/11, a difference being that a third of the hundred-thousand-plus people of Japanese ancestry who lived in Los Angeles were Nisei, citizens of Japan, and most of whom were followers of Shintoism, the national religion of Japan. They had been taught from the time they were born that their emperor was a deity, a direct descendant of the sun. Even though many of them were also Buddhists, all of them had been schooled in obedience to Emperor Hirohito. Kamikaze pilots destroyed thirty-four American ships and damaged 368 others by turning their Zeros into human-guided missiles. In the Pacific they killed 4,900 sailors and wounded 4,800 more. Religious fanaticism is a deadly military force, and it is not only pilots who have religion. It

Vegetable concession in wholesale produce market, operated almost exclusively by residents of Japanese ancestry before they were evacuated, Photo: Clem Albers 1942, Berkeley Library, B-43

cannot be difficult to believe that the military men in California recommended to the Secretary of War that President Roosevelt do something about the hosts of people along our west coast who might feel a stronger allegiance to their ancestors and their emperor than to the American people who had refused them citizenship and land ownership.

Nisei owned choice land that they farmed, no ordinary property. I remember from early childhood seeing the rolling green hills above the highway where hundreds of Japanese farmers labored over nearly all of the vegetables that Mother Wood overcooked and forced me to eat. Investors probably looked at those green hills another way entirely, coveting the land for future real estate development. I have no doubt that the voices of land speculators were among those "hysterical" petitioners for the removal of the Japanese Americans.

Every school child in Los Angeles probably knew a Sachiko or Hiro, and the Japanese kids I knew were admirable, good students, respected both by their teachers and their peers. We also knew that our Japanese classmates went to school on Saturday to learn the language and customs of their ancestors. That seemed particularly odd to me at the time. In my own experience, every day had a specified purpose. Just as Monday was always washday for Mother Wood and weekdays were always school days for me, weekends were universally special. Saturday, the original Sabbath, was now a family day and, because Sunday was the day that Jesus arose from the dead, Sunday was the Christian Sabbath. In our opinion, "American" children did not go to school on Saturday.

Most of us were sad to know they had to leave. When Horace Mann Junior High School's student body president was plucked out of school to be sent off to an "assembly center," before being put on a train headed east, no one thought he was our enemy. But I suspect that few of us understood anything of his sadness, his humiliation, or the shock of knowing he was no longer regarded as a real American. He had been disenfranchised. Everything he had always supposed about his own status had suddenly been stripped from him. And after 9/11, we saw that same sudden alienation in the wake of "The War on Terror." Muslims living in the United States, whether citizens or not, who have raised their families to be both devout and model citizens have become suspect. It is true that we have not displaced the Muslims among us from their homes, but that may be because they are among us, not surrounding our harbors. All we do is suspect them, possibly glare at them, or simply avoid them.

* * *

I don't think I learned much of anything that was true during the war. It didn't touch me much directly. I only knew one person who was killed, and I didn't know him very well. His name was Palmer. I went to his wedding at a Salvation Army Mission. He had married Patsy, a woman Mr. and Mother Wood befriended because she was somehow related to Mr. Wood and had lived much of her life in an institution for mentally impaired people. I heard Mother Wood tell someone that Patsy had been "fixed," meaning that she had been sterilized. I remember the wedding. We sat in folding chairs in a rather bare room, possibly a storefront. Patsy looked very happy hanging on to Palmer's arm. I thought she almost looked pretty. Something different from her usual crooked half smile. Palmer was taller than she was. I thought he was sort of nice looking. He was wearing a suit.

Palmer was a paperboy, not the kind that used to ride a bicycle and throw the *Herald Express* onto the Woods' front porch, but the kind who wove through downtown traffic, yelling, "Extra! Extra! Read all about it!" when he stopped at a signal.

Mother Wood worried about him. It was such dangerous work. "What would become of poor Patsy if anything happened to him?"

Not long after the wedding, Mother Wood gave Patsy a half-grown fox terrier that someone at church was trying to find a good home for. Mother Wood had been thinking that Patsy needed something to take care of since she couldn't have a baby. Palmer thought it was a good idea too. He said that Patsy would just start crying for no reason at all. The day we took the dog over, Patsy had invited the family to dinner. I dimly remember their house as being about the size of a big garage. It was hidden from the street by a tired looking two-story frame. I don't remember anything about the dinner except the huge pile of string beans on Palmer's plate.

That's all I ever knew about Palmer. A short time before I went to Denver, I heard that he had been drafted into the marines. He had gone through seven or eight weeks of basic training before being sent to the South Pacific, to some little island. Mother Wood couldn't think of the name. I don't know whether Palmer ever learned it. It didn't really matter much. He was killed going ashore.

Mother Wood said it was a shame but that he had died for his country. To me, at fifteen, it made no sense at all, served no purpose. To me, at eighty-three, it seems an even greater evil, because I realize he never counted to anyone but Patsy and Patsy didn't count either. Their barren, separate lives were hardly noticed.

Coda

In the dissenting opinion in the case testing the constitutionality of the executive order, Justice Frank Murphy referred to the Commanding General's Final Report on the evacuation:

> That this forced exclusion was the result in good measure of this erroneous assumption of racial guilt rather than bona fide military necessity is evidenced by the Commanding General's Final Report on the evacuation from the Pacific Coast area. In it he refers to all individuals of Japanese descent as "subversive," as belonging to "an enemy race" whose "racial strains are undiluted," and as constituting "over 112,000 potential enemies at large today" along the Pacific Coast.

The relocation camps were wrong and dehumanizing, but they were far from being analogous to Germany's concentration camps. They were not created as a step in the extermination of a group of people. They were created by the military as an expedient solution to both actual and projected problems, in an atmosphere that fostered fear and injustice: war against an enemy nation that had just destroyed most of our Pacific Fleet while its emissaries were in Washington. Long before Pearl Harbor, the United States had demonstrated its hostility toward immigrants in general and Asians in particular. Fear, greed, and expediency all led to Roosevelt's Executive Order 9066, and easy identification made it enforceable. The removal from coastal areas of loyal, even native-born Americans and their immigrant parents, and transfer of their hard-earned wealth to those ready to exploit them, while allowing less visible Nazi sympathizers, German Bund members, to remain in their California homes was unconscionable.

1942 DENVER AND MY PEOPLE

The train ride to Denver was very different from my earlier trip to Billings. The coach was full of soldiers. I sat next to a lone sailor. He had a nice face. I was crying as the train left Los Angeles, trying not to because I usually tried not to. I don't remember much about the landscape. I stared at the sailor's watch.

"It's a chronometer," he said.

"A what?"

"A chronometer...see these little buttons? I can use it like a stopwatch, or I can tell how fast the train is moving." He said that he was from Denver and that I would like it there, better than Los Angeles, and that the skies were blue and I would probably ski in the nearby mountains. He managed to make me feel less frightened by giving me a glimpse of my destination, so that I was not just riding a train to the edge of the earth.

When he went off somewhere to drink, or play cards, or just talk to someone who was not a child, a pink-faced soldier who'd been sitting on the floor at the back of the overcrowded coach took the seat beside me. He had a deck of cards. Because cards were things of the devil, I had not seen a deck since I left Billings, and had forgotten the names of the suits,

WWII chronograph, similar to the one worn by the sailor I sat next to on my train ride to Denver, 1942, permission granted by Montres DOXA, SA

so he soon gave up the task of teaching me a rummy game, and we talked, or he did.

His grammar was "bad," and I disliked him for it, just as I disliked his rumpled uniform and thin blond hair. Still, when he offered his shoulder for me to rest against, I accepted, and when he put his arm around me, I did not object. He said it was a lot more comfortable that way. I dozed off, alternately lulled by the rhythm of the train and roused by the unexpected.

Slowly, very slowly, his hand fell closer to my breast, and because it was happening so slowly, I was more aware of the pleasant feeling in my own body than I was of the purposefulness of the move, so that by the time his hand had fumbled its way inside my blouse, I had no desire whatsoever to ask him to remove it. While I felt that what I was allowing to happen was wrong, I saw no reason that that should preclude my enjoyment. In fact, the complete disgust probably enhanced my enjoyment, so that I was quite receptive to the advance of his other hand into my underpants. It felt very good and very bad.

But the sailor came back, shoved me as though to wake me, and told the soldier to find another seat. The next day, the sailor taught me the card suits, accompanied me to the diner for every meal, and pointed out the railroad cars on sidings, sitting in isolation in the empty West. He said, "Japanese who have been evacuated will go to Utah and Colorado as soon as there are places for them."

That seemed reasonable enough to me. I knew that they weren't all enemies, saboteurs, spies, but I had been told that it was necessary. I wish that I could say that I had thought it was unjust. I wish that I could even say that the sailor with the kind face and the wonderful chronometer thought it was unjust. Now, I wonder if even if they had been taking those carloads of people to cyanide showers, would I have known, or anyone on our train have known, or worse, had we known would it be possible that we would have accepted that, too?

Mother had a war job and was at work when my train arrived in Denver. The twins met me. As always, I had come at the wrong time. Mother had just recovered from years of grieving over Juneau's death and had reentered the world; Mardie was involved with an older, married man; Cynthia was in the terminal stages of a marriage to an older man; and Neil was about to marry a Mexican woman who "could not possibly be good enough" for him, who in all probability considered him a "very fine catch, indeed," as Mother put it. And there I came, with a sailor and a soldier, a cheap suitcase, my wrists jutting from my outgrown jacket, my shoes cracking under layers of white polish. Stinking. I could smell the accumulated sweat of two-and-a-half unwashed days. It seemed to me, when I was fifteen I always smelled of either ripe sweat or old menstrual blood, and that day, in the heat of the coach I had kept my arms pinned to my side, because each movement I made appalled me.

I was among nice people. Mardie hugged me and said how glad she was to finally have her baby sister come home. Cynthia took me home with her, to a luxurious bath, with all the hot water I wanted, bath salts, perfumed soap, and thick, monogrammed towels. It was not at all like the scrubbing I had received when I returned to Los Angeles from Montana. It was like a baptism, a renewal, a welcome.

Cynthia helped me find some presentable clothes among the things I had brought, at the same time making it rather clear that most of the things in my suitcase were not quite right...for Denver.

I was ready to meet my mother, the tall, willowy woman in Mother Wood's myth, in my own. But she was shorter than I, a little dumpy in her slacks. Almost sixty. The voice was the same, and the mouth, and her black eyes brimming with tears. I didn't want her to cry, I didn't want her to call me Darling, and I didn't want her to kiss me. It was all inevitable, and I must have recoiled, because she said, "You *still* don't like Mother, do you?" At least I didn't run from her, and I didn't call her "Mrs. McKenzie," even though it came quickly to my lips, while "Mother" stuck in my throat like a fishbone.

We all went out to dinner, my glamorous sisters, my too-loud mother, and I. I had come into a whole new world that surpassed any dream I had of the way life might be. The truth was that I had never known anything of the way life might be, so it had not really been possible to dream—and certainly I did not yet know. I had just gone from a small, dark chamber into a somewhat larger one. I was to be born again and again.

MAMMY
DEC. 31, 194

1943 SISTERHOOD

By spring of 1943, when I arrived in Denver, Mardie had become the buyer for the Young Denver Shop at the Denver Dry Goods Company. Mother had recently taken a wartime civil service job as a clerk at Lowry Field. Early in WWII, Lowry had become the US Army Air Forces Training Command, charged with training fifty-seven thousand soldiers a year. While the base brought welcome jobs and business to Denver, the flood of military families filled every available living space. Mother was sharing Mardie's one-bedroom apartment at the Robert Browning, an apartment low-rise in Capitol Hill's Poet's Row. Obviously, there was no room for me.

Cynthia had room. She had married Walter Koch on the nineteenth of July 1941. In her yearbook, Mother noted, *Cynthia and Walter were married at 4:00 p.m. in the chapel at the Episcopal Church. Sweet family wedding. They went to Colo Sprs [sic] and are going on a trip for two or three weeks.*

In early April of 1941, Mother had written that Cynthia had resigned her Mountain Bell job. Walter Koch was a middle-aged widower with two children and Cynthia was his twenty-four-year-old secretary. (Because I, like nature herself, abhor a vacuum, I have to fill in every blank. I suspect,

Drawing I did of my mother a couple of years after arriving in Denver

Cynthia standing in front of her house, circa 1940

but don't know, that her personal relationship with her boss wobbled his ladder to the presidency of the company.) Mother once described the pair as a perfect couple. She recalled watching them as they walked away from her toward his Aston-Martin or whatever it was. They were going to the Denver Country Club. Walter was "so tall" and Cynthia was "so svelte, with those narrow hips."

I spent my first few nights in Denver at Cynthia's house. I remember the beautiful drive up Seventh Avenue Parkway. It was May. Tulips were everywhere—and lilacs, both rare in Los Angeles. We stopped in front of a two-story brick house on Ash Street. I don't remember what I had expected, but I was surprised that Cynthia lived in such a nice house, in what I perceived as a "fancy" neighborhood. I was even more surprised when she opened the front door. We didn't walk right into the living room. There was an entrance hall with a coat closet on one side and a small table on the other. The living room furniture was pretty, but not inviting. It didn't look very comfortable to me. There wasn't even a davenport or an over-stuffed chair, just silk upholstered chairs and a velvet couch—like the furniture in magazines, and the big dollhouse at the museum in Exposition Park. In fact, the entire house was different in every way from the Woods' five-room frame house on West Seventieth Street, the one I'd lived in most of my life. Cynthia's place had all sorts of rooms: a foyer, a den, a powder room, a pantry, a laundry room, and a master bedroom that was bigger than the Woods' living room and dining room combined. The bedroom was so big that it even had extra furniture.

Meaning to show my own taste and sophistication, I said that I really liked her "chase lounge."

"Oh, the *chaise longue*?" Cynthia said. "It's very comfortable, just right for reading." That was only my first French lesson. I quickly learned to fear seeming to be *naïve*, but that was at least forgivable; being *gauche* was not. *Bourgeois* taste was a bad thing to have. Being *nouveau riche* was even worse. Mardie and Mother didn't live in a cramped little apartment. It was just a *pied-à-terre*. I had many occasions to perfect my pronunciation of *faux pas*.

Just being in the presence of such *savoir faire* and luxury made me feel like a princess. Of course, I knew that I wasn't, just as I had known nine years before that I hadn't actually been born again. I couldn't help imagining how wonderfully happy Cynthia's life was and I tried desperately to appear to fit in. She was glamorous. She knew exactly how to speak and act in every situation. She had a wonderful husband, a wonderful house, filled with wonderful things. She lived in a wonderful neighborhood. I thought it was no wonder she had so much *aplomb*!

That night, I slept in Cynthia's bed, next to Cynthia. She said she hoped I didn't mind that arrangement. She apologized, saying that usually her guests stayed in the guest room but Walter, her husband, had taken it over. He could sleep better there. She said that it was all right with her because she didn't like to listen to him snore.

I stayed at Cynthia's for several days, while Mardie continued to look for a larger place, one that would accommodate both Mother and me. During my stay, I saw Walter only once, fleetingly. I believe he nodded at me, nothing more. I met his daughters, Wanda and Ellen, shortly after I arrived. Cynthia introduced me as her little sister, Meegie, and told them I would be enrolling at East High School, the same school they attended. Both were courteous, even friendly. Ellen said that East High was great and that maybe we would be in some of the same classes.

Cynthia probably made breakfast for me every morning during my stay, but I only remember one. I was sitting in the sunny little breakfast room, eating rice pancakes that my sister had made especially for me. She had slathered half a stick of rationed butter on them, and I had baptized them in maple syrup, poured from a Log Cabin tin. I had only taken a bite or two when I heard a scream from the kitchen. Suddenly Wanda was standing in the breakfast room, waving a Kellogg's box and crying. The night before, Cynthia, apparently out of spite, had poured water into every box of breakfast cereal in the house, leaving Wanda and her sister, Ellen, nothing to eat for breakfast.

The perfect woman who lived in a perfect house in a perfect world was a witch. My response at the time was embarrassment or even guilt. I knew I shouldn't have been sitting in the breakfast room enjoying a lovely breakfast, while legitimate members of the household rummaged in the kitchen for cornflakes. Nor should I have witnessed something so private. I'm sure I just looked away, as though I hadn't noticed. I never mentioned the incident to Cynthia or anyone else, but I had learned something about my sister that I would never forget.

Fortunately for everyone, Cynthia and Walter's marriage only lasted two years. A day or so after the undigested breakfast, Mardie asked me if Cynthia had mentioned that she and Walter were getting a divorce. She added that they had an interlocutory decree and that the divorce wouldn't be final until sometime in the fall. She said I shouldn't mention it. Had it been the sort of question one answers, I might have said no, that the only reference to divorce was on that pretty, lilac-and-tulip-filled drive up Seventh Avenue, when Cynthia had said something completely baffling: "If anyone ever brings up the subject, just say that Mother got a Mexican divorce." I didn't know what "the subject" was; I didn't know what an interlocutory decree was; I didn't know what a Mexican divorce was. Even now, as I write this, trying my best to "Tell it like it is," the one thing I'm sure about is that the day my narrow-hipped sister walked out of the Koch household for the last time, no one but Mother hoped the perfect couple could still work things out.

Under the circumstances, everyone agreed that I would be more comfortable staying at the apartment with Mardie and Mother. Mardie said that the couch in the living room was very comfortable, according to her boyfriend, Jim Hover, who had slept there occasionally.

Cynthia and I remained lifelong friends, more tolerant than close, but she was never unkind to me, at least not directly. Once, when I was eighteen and suffering from the feverish, obsessive, delusional state we refer to as "being in love," I discovered her being entirely too kind to Gerry, my fiancé. She wasn't in bed with him, but he wasn't fighting her off exactly. They were kissing behind the house where Gerry was supposedly helping her retrieve her keys. His betrayal infuriated me. Overall, though, she was much more than a satisfactory older sister.

My first year in Denver, Cynthia and I sat through nearly every movie that came to town. Whether it was her intention or not, she provided me with a crash course in popular culture. I had only seen a handful of movies in my life. I had heard names like Joan Crawford, Bette Davis, Dorothy Lamour, Cary Grant, Tyrone Power, Ronald Reagan, Ginger Rogers, and Fred Astaire, but without Cynthia, I would not have been able to pair the names with their faces and I myself would have been either a nameless face or a faceless name in my new school. I would have been a "who's she?" Cynthia taught me everything that was *de rigueur*. She taught me how to play cards: gin rummy, bridge, and solitaire. Both she and Mardie tried to teach me how to dance, but I always danced to a different drummer. I learned the steps but not the cadence of the foxtrot and I never learned to follow. Cynthia was lithe, graceful as a cat, and she could melt right into her partner, then, quick as a cat, retreat.

By age sixteen, I was an accomplished smoker. Cynthia taught me exactly how to hold a cigarette and order a cocktail, invaluable skills at East High. I never did learn how to hold my liquor though, and just when I thought I was having the time of my life, I would find myself groping a wall on the way to the powder room. I had no idea at the time what a blessing it was to retch over a toilet if I drank another drop after noticing what a wonderful party it was. My McKenzie siblings were to become alcoholics, to a one, being able to drink excessively from the start with relative ease.

Cynthia's daughter Shannon recently described her mother as a hermit, very private. I think everyone who knew Cynthia for any time at all would have said, at least once, that she was difficult. Mardie said she was impossible. I saw Cynthia as aloof, even haughty at times, and yes, difficult, but there was something about that pose that I admired—no, loved. When I first came to Colorado, I had no idea at all why, in the middle of a seemingly convivial holiday meal, she would suddenly stand up, place her napkin on the table, get her coat, gloves, and handbag, raise her chin and, without a word, walk out the door. I still don't.

As I write, I keep trying to understand the people and events that I didn't understand as they happened. Alas, that ends up being just about everything. I never really understood Cynthia because I was always looking for her in the wrong place. I have always seen her as she was in that breakfast room, or at the dining-room table, or sitting through a movie with me. This morning, I thought about her isolation, and Shannon seeing her as a hermit. I remembered her apparent lack of women friends. I can't imagine Cynthia sitting at a kitchen table with a neighbor, having a cup of coffee and a cigarette, wondering what to fix for dinner. And I can't imagine her having anything to talk about with Mardie. After they'd rerun all the things they could laugh about, they would run into all of the other stuff. Being "womb mates" just wasn't enough. It wasn't that she didn't like women, it was that she would rather read a book or just loll around in her own head than hang around with fools.

The clue came as I thought about those men she been loved by and kept in touch with all of her life. All of them were unattainable. Someone, I really can't remember who it was, told me that Cynthia had very much been in love with a man (I think his name was Jack). They were planning to marry, until he learned that a former (we think) girlfriend was about to have his baby. He did the honorable thing, of course, and Cynthia loved him all the more for his decency. In the years before the war, she and Mardie had both had quite a few boyfriends, some of whom they had each dated, but by the time I came to Denver most of them were just the old friends that they heard news about once in a while. In early 1944, she was involved or maybe in love with a soldier, Martin Fierst, who was in the Tenth Mountain Division, the unit made up largely of skiers from Ivy League schools. Martin was married but claimed to have been separated from his wife before he joined the Army. He said that he still hoped for a reconciliation with his wife after life was normal again, but he and Cynthia, half-jokingly, I think, promised each other that if they were both unattached in five years and still interested in each other, they would get in touch. Five years later, to the day, he called. She took the train to New York shortly after. Three months later she returned to Denver. She had a badly lacerated ankle, which she said had been injured when she stepped off a curbing onto a broken bottle. That was all I ever knew about the rendezvous.

Monsignor Canavan always comes to mind when I think of Cynthia's long-term friends. People who knew them invariably smirk when I mention their friendship. Some even come right out and ask, as though I would actually know, whether they slept together. What I do know is that they were true friends who profited from having each other in their lives. Unfortunately, both were heavy drinkers, but that was not the only thing they had in common. Both were funny and bright, well read, and probably lonely. I know, too, that long after his years at the basilica, he was the parish priest at tiny Mother of God. He was in ill health, suffering from diabetes that had cost him one of his legs. He visited Cynthia in 1972 as she lay dying with her breast cancer in the nursing home on Bluff Street in Boulder. Perhaps he took her confession, or perhaps he took her a little bottle of brandy. I know that he blessed her life. (Monsignor Walter Canavan guided Mother of God from 1969 to 1980, celebrating there his fiftieth anniversary as a priest.)

Another of her good friends was Medill Sarkisian, who imported and sold beautiful art objects. I never met him, but I suspect he, too, enriched her life, filled a void, stirred her imagination. Cynthia was artistic, but she never had a chance to develop her skills. While I was still living at the Woods', she sent me a watercolor of books she had painted inside the library in the McKenzie house. Among Mother's things, I found a little pen and watercolor sketch she had made of me, apparently when I was in Billings. She was resourceful in the way artists are. She used the materials at hand. I will always remember the Christmas tree she decorated with and stars cut from beer cans then pierced with an ice pick, in the style of the tin art of Mexico.

Perhaps if such men had been around for her when she was twenty-two, and she had not lived with her alcoholic aunt and uncle, Isabel and Tommy, for two years and been groomed more for their nasty little world than her own, Cynthia might have enjoyed a lifelong companion. But I think she would have preferred a charming sojourner to a permanent resident. Given a real choice, she could never have been a happy housewife; she had never even met one. What seemed to be affectation at times was. She wasn't made from common clay. She was made almost entirely of recycled fairytales and thirties movies. By the time I knew her, she was a synthesis of Bette Davis, Joan Crawford, a little Vivian Leigh, and a bit of Katherine Hepburn. Cynthia was an artifact with hormones. Given her druthers, she would never have married that pretty white house containing a very important man in a three-piece suit, standing near the top of a corporate ladder. Having found herself in the role of housewife and stepmother, she would rather not have poured water on the cereal of the two adolescents who were standing under the ladder. She would have done what the silvery image of Bette Davis would have done in such a circumstance. She would have poured rat poison instead.

Had she had other opportunities she most likely would have been an artist or writer, living in her own airy loft: very simple; just a view, or good north light streaming in; a few beautiful things. She wasn't a hoarder.

So sitting here, staring at my computer, and realizing I have just slipped into my fiction mode, I'm asking myself why didn't she have better choices? It was then that a sixty-seven-year-old World War II song started playing itself in my head. I was actually sitting next to the flesh and blood Cynthia in the Orpheum Theater, in 1943, on Welton Street, the first time I heard Bette Davis sing it on the screen:

> They're either too young or too old...
> They're either too bald or too bold...
> They're either too grey or too grassy green...
> Tomorrow I'll go hiking with that Eagle Scout unless
> I get a call from grandpa for a snappy game of chess

The twins were born in 1916, just before the United States entered "the war to end all wars." They were twenty-three years old when the eligible young men they had known all their lives began to disappear. From 1940 (when the first peacetime Selective Service Act became law) to 1945, virtually every man they ever knew was either in the service, already married, or old enough to be their father. The original Selective Service Act only required men twenty-one to thirty-five to register, but after the attack on Pearl Harbor, every man from eighteen to sixty-five became eligible—including any man born between 1876 and 1923!

The first men in danger of being drafted were, of course, the young, healthy single men. Few if any of their friends were actually drafted; most volunteered for reserve units in one of the services in order to avoid becoming cannon fodder in the infantry. Those who had already graduated from college almost always went in as officers. Cynthia and the rest of the women her age were "the girls they left behind." A few were young widows. Some fell in love with the married men with children and a deferment that kept them out of the service; others, of course, fell in love with soldiers, single or married, whom they hardly knew, because they all looked just alike, even in their underwear. You picked one out and then you invented him.

Below: Me and Mardie playing a game of Scrabble

1944 BOBBY SOXER IN DENVER

Oh, yes. I had just been born again as a bobby soxer in the glamorous wartime world of the forties. I discovered cigarettes and whiskey and the sense of belonging that comes from having the right wardrobe and a reasonably good deodorant. As never before, I was treated like I belonged, was actually popular. I would later discover that I didn't really. My clothes could be perfect, but my story was just not going to fly in the long term.

Besides the clothes and the deodorant, I had a myth. Elizabeth Janeway suggests that myth is our way of bridging the gaps and justifying the discrepancies in history. Personal myth must work that way too. My myth concerned my father. What I knew of him was very little, only what people who had known him were willing to tell me and image shards from my very early childhood, when I had known him by his first name, a big, blond man in white flannel pants, who drove me around in the front seat of his roadster, and who showed up from time to time, for no particular reason. In Billings, Juneau and Mardie had been surprised and amused that I thought Daddy Wood was my father, and Mother had said it was just too funny. Except for the laughter at my ignorance, it was not a matter of much importance, because it had never occurred to me that I needed a

Me, dressed for the prom, 1944

father, particularly since the designation of who was and who was not one's parent seemed to me quite arbitrary.

In Denver, I picked up more information. I learned that he was years younger than my mother, and that she had apparently loved him a great deal more than he had loved her, so she was still very angry with him. According to my mother's myth, he was living in Mexico City on his second wife's money, providing rather generously for his present mistress's keep. "That son-of-a-bitch," she would say. "He was going to do so much for you. Nothing would be too good for you. Not a dime."

I learned that, because he was not allowed on the Woods' property (not only that, much later, my half-sister Daphne told me that Mother had a restraining order against him that prevented him getting any closer), the real purpose of that car conversation with Mardie was to allow my father a chance to see me as he stood at the end of the block and that other times he would "stand at a distance" to watch me play. And that the mysterious man who wanted to talk with me on the phone once, while I was still at the Wood's, who had a boyish voice, was my father. But there was nothing to say.

Out of that, I constructed a father who was brilliant, impetuous, loving, and rich. He was probably as real to me as anyone else's father was to them, and with him and a certain amount of evasion I was as respectable as anyone else at my new school. Although Cynthia had cautioned, "If anyone asks, just say that Mother got a Mexican divorce," no one asked, any more than I asked anyone about their parents' marital status, nor cared. But it seemed to me that I was living a lie, that I myself had been born not only a bastard but a liar and a fraud. It was quite a long time later that I finally realized that anyone who would dislike me solely on the grounds that my mother had tried unsuccessfully, or perhaps too successfully, to be a flapper at age forty-three, was not worth my interest and would make an exceedingly dull friend.

There was something else about myself that I tried very hard to hide, almost as hard as I tried to discover it. I seemed always to like females better than males, or maybe it wasn't even that. I think I did like boys, but I was less successful in my relationships with them than I was with girls. Though I dated a reassuring number of boys, the time I spent with them was usually empty, disappointing. I was inept at all of the games, boring

Senior year portrait

and bored. I tried to appear sophisticated by smoking Lucky Strikes in a cigarette holder. I attempted to be amusing but became known as sarcastic. My idea of conversation was a kind of verbal ping-pong, in which a pause was a missed point. The game was over before I even learned to hold the paddle.

I yearned for true love, some magic moment which would change the course of my life. I studied Katherine Hepburn and Ingrid Bergman far more intently than I studied Latin and chemistry. Immediately after seeing *For Whom the Bell Tolls,* I cropped my hair, hoping the scissors would transform me into a Bergman. I liked my boyish image in the mirror.

I yearned for a career, for recognition. I wanted to write brilliant novels, full of insights about other people, not ordinary, dull books with

Me (second row, left) and my Denver girlfriends, 1944

excess words, but books my millions of readers would not be able to put down, books with my own wisdom, polished to perfection. Mother said that all writers used plot wheels, with each spoke a sensational (though common and predictable) turn of events to randomly create a storyline, very mechanical. She said that she herself had written most of my father's screenplays. She thought it was likely that I had inherited genius from both sides. Plot wheels were a device. I puzzled over the problem of choosing one of eight or twelve set plots for my life story.

The first person to befriend me when I started to East High School was Barbara Bernstein, a lovely girl who Miss Sparhawk, the dean of girls, assigned to help new students feel at home. Most students performing this task did so in a perfunctory way, but Barbara was too genuine to simply introduce me to one or two classmates, show me where the lavs were and point out the cafeteria. She ate lunch with me and included me in her circle of friends. One day, I took her downtown to meet my wonderful sister, the buyer in the college shop at the Denver Dry. I just knew Mardie would be pleased to see that I had made friends so quickly. I was stunned when she whisked me into her office and told me not to hang around with Jews, "The other kids will think you are Jewish." I am deeply ashamed and saddened to this day that I soon began avoiding Barbara, even though I had enjoyed her friendship and I had no idea why being mistaken for a Jew was such a bad thing. Every time Barbara caught my eye as I ate lunch at another table or I tried to ignore her as I passed her in the hall, I learned a deeper lesson; what it meant to betray a friend, to be a Judas. I do hope she had better friends than me, worthy of her truly superior nature.

I next made friends with an orphan, a maverick who cut school with me every Friday, who said in the course of every conversation "Take it easy," and grinned. She had a classically beautiful face, hair as short as mine, and wore Levis every minute she was not in school. I loved Velda Grunwwald, a.k.a. "Mugsy." We decided to get a mountain job together, waiting on tables at a lodge. We were pleased to share a room and the lumpy double bed, whose mattress smelled of dust. The springs sagged, rolling us to the middle, so it was not possible to keep apart for the entire night; and I was always aware of the touching, pleased by it, ashamed of my pleasure. One night, a moth got under the sheet, fluttering and bumping until I rolled over on it. I could feel it for a long time against my flesh, beating like an irregular pulse, so I didn't move, fearing it would fly into my face. In the morning, still knowing it was there, I eased off of it, to find it dead and gray and harmless. That same night I let the greasy headwaiter kiss me.

By the time I was eighteen I was no longer afraid of moths and had outgrown my adolescent preference for females. Still, I wondered what those shorthaired, swaggering women that I sometimes saw walking hand in hand on Colfax Avenue did. I tried to imagine. I wondered if I was one of them, and then I thanked God that I wasn't.

I had a great social life at East High but in 1944, it was as close to a girls' school as a public high school could be. I heard rumors about them, the missing boys from the class of '45, the classmates who had entered college early in hope of qualifying for officer's training. Or if they entered a profession that General Hershey deemed crucial, they might qualify for a deferment.

At the time, I didn't think of our Friday-night potlucks as having anything to do with our missing classmates. We weren't part of "the Greatest Generation." We were the bobby soxers, the little sisters who allegedly swooned over Frank Sinatra. We adored Van Johnson. We yearned to be Ingrid Bergman or Lauren Bacall. Our war was on the silver screen. Our heroes were handsome and clean and they only killed people who deserved to die. We weren't left behind. We were left out. But we were patriotic. We had paper drives. We saved bacon grease for making nitroglycerin. We bought war bonds.

Our crowd knew how to make the best of it. Usually ten or twelve girls would show up for Friday-Night Potluck with a small contribution to a meal whose main course was provided by invisible hands in the kitchen. (Who did fix those nice casseroles?) The two or three girls who actually had steady boyfriends usually got picked up right after dinner. The rest of us would hang around and play bridge or go with a small group to a neighborhood theater—usually the Esquire or the Bluebird. I never had a date pick me up after Potluck, but I couldn't have cared less. It was easier to bid a hand of bridge than talk to a date who didn't know me at all but thought I had a "swell personality" because I shoved my test paper way over to the left of my desk so he could see the answer. At the end of the test, I couldn't sign the oath that I had neither given nor received help. Later, he told my best friend that I shouldn't wear such baggy sweaters.

Like twin fairy godmothers, my sisters outfitted me for my first prom. Mardie supplied the dress and the garnet necklace. The problem was, I didn't know any boys. I knew lots of girls, but no boys. Cynthia supplied my date, a young soldier with a wonderful name, Hunt Norris. He was too old for me and too young for Cynthia, but he was charming. He had told Cynthia he was the son of Kathleen Norris, then, having caught Cynthia's attention, he quickly admitted that his mother was not *the* Kathleen Norris. He had been in pursuit of Cynthia when she shanghaied him and forced him, by whatever means, to take her little sister to her first prom.

By twelfth grade, most of my friends and I began dating college boys, not those smart boys who had abandoned East High to enter college, but rich, mostly 4F (classified as unfit by Selective Service) fraternity boys. I went out with a boy who had asked the mother of a friend to introduce him to me. Such a gentleman! His name was Alston, or Bud, but he preferred to be called Hoser. He liked to say witty things like, "If she's cute, the Hoser knows 'er." His father owned the Ford distributorship for the state of Colorado. His father belonged to the Denver Country Club. My mother thought he was a nice catch. I really couldn't stand him. For one thing, he had a fat bottom.

1945 Looking for My Father

Before I enrolled at the University of Denver I went to Los Angeles, where I made an eighteen-year-old's version of a search for my father. It is probably no coincidence that I fell in love with Gerry very shortly after my return. I had gone to California because Daddy Wood was very sick and had asked to see me. It was the first that I knew that he cared about me at all. For most of my childhood, he had been away, or under his car, or behind the newspaper. He was, like my real, mythic father, all clothes and cars. He worked at the telephone company as a chauffeur; his regular job was to drive the vice president of the company around the state and to drive visiting dignitaries to places that dignitaries go. He was a small man, vain about his appearance. His closet was full of tailor-made suits, polished Florsheim shoes, and a row of hats for all suits and seasons. Occasionally, a visiting vice president would mistake him for another person of value, and Daddy Wood would tell about the incident at Sunday dinner, chuckling and repeating the exchange.

Sometimes on summer evenings, when his long workday left enough daylight to filter through the lace curtains, he would take his mandolin down from the top of the player piano and play a lively piece or two, more

My father, right, with Spencer Tracy, during filming of Quick Millions, *1931*

like a banjo player than a mandolin player. After the joyful flurry, he would return the instrument to its place, again to become an inert thing beside the blond, sweet Jesus and the silver-plated horse. Those times when he, occasionally, came in with liquor on his breath, Mother Wood would detect it before the screen door banged shut. He would say, motioning toward me, "Shh...shh...just one little glass of wine," but later, always after I was in bed, there would be loud voices, and Mother Wood would cry. I would yearn to console her.

Once, in fact, I went, full of righteousness and love, into the living room to throw my arms around her. She yelled, "Go to bed and stay there and don't get out of bed until you are told to."

Just before I left California, he came home with a black, ill-cut suit and a cap, not the sort of cap he liked to wear on Saturdays, but a black cap that matched the suit, that is, a uniform that identified him as a servant. The new regime at the telephone company was perhaps influenced by the war, where it was necessary to make a clear distinction between officers and enlisted men. Mr. Wood was no longer to be mistaken for a "person of value."

When I arrived from Denver, he was very glad to see me, and very tearful, very helpless. We didn't have much to say to each other. Sadly, it was only a few days before my own desire to do good, not just by being there for Mr. Wood, but to fit into the family, faded, along with Mother Wood's patience. She had thought I was coming back to stay, to go to work at the telephone company, but she was soon reminded of my sulkiness, and she discovered that I smoked. I told her, actually. She took that considerably better than she took the news that I was going to try to find my biological father.

I got on a bus and went to the corner of Hollywood and Vine, which was all I knew of Hollywood. I went into a drugstore and began calling people and places Mother had mentioned in connection with my father, just names, actually, and most of the time there were several people by the same name and I never found the right one. Truthfully, I expected him to walk into that drugstore and recognize me as his beloved daughter. I drank a limeade, waited, made more calls, anonymously, mysteriously, until I talked to a woman at the Screen Director's Guild who said, "He's not a director; he's just a writer." I was out of nickels. I took my bus token and returned to the Woods. The rest of my stay there consisted of backing out gracefully.

Owl Rexall Pharmacy where I made my call to the Screen Actor's Guild, postcard

1946 Coeditus Interruptus

When I was eighteen I realized that love was a temporary state, an illusion, and that it interfered with the real purpose of life. I did not intend to fall in love, and I certainly did not wish to get married. I was going to do something better with my life, something important. I knew that writing was much more intricate than using a plot wheel. That approach was for hacks. I knew that I would need to study psychology, so that I would know exactly why people behaved the ways that they did. And I knew that I would have to study English, so that I could write perfect sentences, so that I could manipulate language.

Knowing all of this, I enrolled at the University of Denver, where I took English, psychology, physics, and zoology. I believed that all students remained anonymous, even in the relatively small classes at DU. ("Tramway Tech" it was called then because of the streetcar line.) I also believed that I was supposed to know everything that I knew I didn't know, so if I wasted my money actually buying the required textbook, someone might suspect that I didn't already know all that was worth knowing. In 1946, I thought I was far too wonderful to take Tramway Tech seriously. I was not there to learn; I was there to transfer to University of

University of Denver, a.k.a. "Tramway Tech," immediately after WWII, circa 1946

Colorado with enough credits to stay even with my old friends from East High. At the time, I was miffed because two years in a row my mother had allowed me to enroll at CU, and even agreed I could share a dorm room with a friend, before deciding she couldn't afford the room and board. I'm pretty sure she really couldn't.

I'm also fairly certain I was not a good risk. I might have been, had Mother ever shown any interest in what I was doing at school but never in my high school career did she ask to see one of my report cards. I interpreted that as meaning high school was unimportant. As I write, it dawns on me that she put off telling me she didn't have the money for CU because she was waiting, or hoping, to hear from Chaunce, who had vowed he would send me to college. He probably couldn't afford the tuition either but didn't want to admit it.

I lived to regret never completing the freshman English composition requirement at DU. My one quarter of charming my composition teacher netted me nothing—as in nothing will come of nothing. I wrote several poems, which I thought were quite beautiful, and submitted them in place of the dull, prose compositions the teacher had required. When I read them in front of my English class, the other freshman thought they were profound, in their sighing of the relentlessness of the sea, the evanescence of moments. My kind but gullible teacher apologized for the B she gave me; she said that she loved my poetry, but...well, I had just missed so many classes. (Uh, yeah, I had twenty-two cuts. I mean, I made time in my busy schedule to attend eight of the classes.)

My young psychology teacher turned out to be less forgiving and really rather canny. The class was a mere rerun of my high school psychology course, so I didn't bother buying the book and attended only on quiz days. The teacher waited until the last day of the quarter to say, "Well, hello, Miss Brown. I see you have shown up for the quiz again." He knew me. He gave me a D.

I aced the physics class though. I had attended because it didn't interfere with anything important, like lunch. The professor, Byron Cohen, designed a class especially for coeds, because, who knows? Someday the pretty little things might need to know that every action has a reaction and/or understand the multiple meanings of gravity and levity.

I had a better attitude toward the zoology class. It was a premed class. It wasn't that I hoped to become a doctor. I knew that was not only unlikely but undesirable. My own fatherly family physician referred to the few women in his profession as "hen medics." I heard a Chi Psi joke about his being interviewed for a faculty position by a woman (with six kids) whom he described as being "a man with undescended testicles." I took zoology because I was so late for registration that it was the only class still open. Besides, I loved science. My limited options were only partially the result of arrogance and lassitude. The war had ended just four months before, and the thousands of veterans suddenly enrolling in school completely overwhelmed college campuses. They had all but emptied the

Old Main, University of Denver, where I met my husband in a zoology class, Photo: University of Denver, https://creativecommons.org/licenses/by-nc-sa/4.0/

DU bookstore and by the time I wandered in there wasn't a single zoology text left.

The zoology class was on the third floor of Old Main. I thought the concave maple treads on the stairs were worn to maybe a sixteenth of an inch, too thin to bear my weight. The floors squeaked. It was just my luck to have a class on the third floor of a firetrap. Worse, without thinking, I had taken a seat in the front row near the door just before the professor passed around the seating chart, meaning I was stuck in that seat for the quarter. I was especially annoyed because some dope behind me made comments about the two bilaterally symmetric moles on my neck. "Hey, look, she has eyes on the back of her neck." I didn't bother to turn around and demonstrate my actual glare.

He was probably the same goon who bumped me out of his way as he rushed toward the student union for lunch. I had to wait for Barbara Young, who sat at the back of the room. By the time we got to the student union, the cafeteria line extended out the door and down the stairs. The only empty table in the lunchroom had a book on it, but Barbara noticed that it was a zoology book and said, "Someone from our class!" We had just seated ourselves when the owner of the book showed up. Before either of us could say that we hoped he didn't mind, he began unloading his full tray. He just waved or maybe shrugged and sat down, suggesting that we get in line because the cafeteria was running out of everything.

What I remember most about that half-hour lunch was listening to Barbara's skillful grilling of the guy while I was thinking that, with the exception of his white-sidewall-haircut and too-short pants, he was nice looking—handsome, in fact. He told Barbara that he was in premed, planning to be a neurosurgeon; he'd been a naval aviator, a fighter pilot on a jeep carrier. Barbara said her fiancé was also a fighter pilot, still in the Army Air Corps Reserve. I was thinking that all the Navy guy really needed was a decent haircut and a tailor. After I entered the conversation, the main topic was his trousers. He said he was wearing his uniform pants because of the shortage of civilian men's clothes. No, his forestry green trousers didn't identify him as a marine; he had been a naval aviator. The marine and naval cadets all trained together and didn't choose their branch of service until they finished their training. All other naval officers

Gerry, shortly before we met

had four different uniforms: white, khaki, grey, and blue, but naval aviators had a fifth, the green that was also worn by marines. I think I imagined what he would have looked like in each uniform.

I noticed that he had a nice smile, very white teeth, just a bit uneven. When I mentioned not having a zoology text, he told me he had an extra one. He'd bought the text when he decided to go back to school; he wanted to be ready to go when classes started. Then as soon as he enrolled, he had gotten all his books and equipment on the GI Bill. He had an extra slide rule too, if I needed it. He could bring them by the dorm...if he could borrow his brother's car. I said I didn't live in a dorm (DU didn't have dorms yet) but that I had a live-in job babysitting close to the campus. And I wouldn't need the slide rule.

He showed up that very afternoon with the book, just to drop it by. He couldn't stay. He said mom was fixing neck bones for dinner, just for him. He also had to get his brother's car back.

I didn't know his name, just Gerry something, until I saw it written on the flyleaf of the book. Gerald J. McClard. I thought it was a nice name. (Did alliteration cross my mind?) The handwriting was nice too—like his teeth, even but not too even. Casual.

There was a little piece of lined paper sticking out of the top of the book. I thought it was a bookmark saving his place, but it was a note.

On it he'd penciled:

I am just a little amoeba in culture trying to grow.

I eat my fellow phyla wherever I may go.

Into my pseudopodia, my heart and soul do flow.

A Paramecium caudatum *is my gastronomical goal.*

Amusing. Actually, I was kind of getting used to his haircut, and if the moles on my neck had not been blind, they would have recognized the humor in his blue eyes right away.

* * *

Soon I knew a little more than that he was handsome. As a fighter pilot he'd never been in a dogfight. He flew escort, which meant, he explained,

Top: Gerry getting into cockpit of plane

Left: Jeep carrier, like the one Gerry flew from in the Pacific Theater during WWII, USN NS0305704

strafing missions, where they attack ground targets after diving toward them, sometimes civilian targets—villages. Despite his Distinguished Flying Cross he said he was not a hero. Sometimes, before dawn, when they catapulted him off the little jeep carrier, when the seas were so heavy the swells almost met the deck, he would wet his pants in terror. He said that all the young pilots knew they were expendable, a part of the war budget. Sure, he had medals, but they didn't mean anything. He just wanted to get his ass out of there. The war didn't mean anything. He didn't believe there were any heroes.

He said MacArthur was a fake, that the stirring picture of his wading ashore was staged after the battle was over, after the young soldiers had gone ashore, or had been removed from the water to be shipped home. His cynicism shocked me because we at home were all so *patriotic*. I had imagined heroism to be an elevated emotional state of which I, and perhaps every woman, was incapable.

He had wanted to be a doctor from the times he had gone with his mother to the clinic at Denver General Hospital. He had seen *The Magnificent Obsession* three times in one day and decided to become a brain surgeon, to really help people. He also wrote poetry. He said that most of it wasn't very good, but if I'd really like to read it he might be able to find a couple of things he had written in the South Pacific. "Do you know 'Invictus'? That's my favorite. I like 'The Rubaiyat' a lot though." He quoted from both. He was actually *sensitive*.

When we went on dates he wore his dress blues, stripped of the gold braid and gold buttons. He wore a Homburg hat and black, French-toed shoes. "I always wanted a Homburg," he said. Of all the things he had always wanted the hat was certainly the easiest to come by. It turned out he was having some suits tailor-made. He'd always wanted nice clothes.

His family had been poor. Once in first grade, his pants had split open, exposing his bare butt. His humiliation had been complete when the teacher put him across her knee before the class and stuck a safety pin in his pants.

Before I ever saw him in his new suits, wearing his five-dollar pure-silk necktie with a palm tree painted on it, he had given me a diamond ring and a chronic feeling of congestion in my...pudenda. At first, the feeling was the residue of unsatisfactory sex but very soon it was the earliest sign that I was pregnant, one discomfort blending into the next.

* * *

So that's pretty much the way I picked out the father of my children. I didn't know that was what I was doing. I hadn't even thought about being a wife, a housewife, and certainly not a mother. Being a housewife meant doing housework, vacuuming, dusting, scrubbing floors, cleaning toilets, things like that. Being a mother meant taking care of a child. I was not crazy about children. They got on my nerves. They were noisy and troublesome. I knew because I had been working as a live-in babysitter, ironing little

Homburg hat like Gerry wore when we went out on dates

French-toed Florsheim shoes with a thin sole

puffed sleeves, cleaning up messes, giving them baths, putting them to bed, reading the same bedtime stories over and over. I didn't even consider actually having a baby; I mean giving birth. I was almost certain I would not be able to do that, at least I hoped not. More than once I wondered if my aversion to all those womanly tasks meant that I was weird, you know, queer. On the other hand, I didn't really understand why being female meant being doomed to a lifetime of toilet cleaning. Maybe I had the wrong hormones, but I knew I wouldn't make a good man either. I would have hated shaving and I would have been a coward in war. I hated the very idea of war. Cleaning toilets was better than being cannon fodder.

As for Lieutenant, junior grade, G. J. McClard, United States Navy Reserve: he was finally home from that other world. Back home. But that isn't exactly what he had been dreaming about and saving his money for. What he and his friend Lt. j.g. G.J. McCormick USNR, "Mac" (they called each other Mac), had always planned to do after the war was pool their money, all that money they had earned but couldn't spend. They were going to buy a sailboat, probably a used one would be all they could afford. They were going to get it in shape, and the two of them were going to sail around the world, maybe even to some of those little islands in the South Pacific, where the natives had red teeth from chewing betel nuts. They were going to get away from the whole lousy so-called civilized world and start their lives over a day at a time. But even before Mac was discharged from the Navy, he had married Marge, his old girlfriend from South High School. And when the war was finally over they had come back to Denver. As Gerry put it, "She already had one in the oven." Gerry had been at Fitzsimons Army Hospital, in the waiting room with Mac when the baby was born, red and wrinkled with a funny-shaped head. Mac was going to go back to school and Marge would work part time. They were going to live in one of the Quonset huts, a decommissioned military half-pipe structures made from corrugated steel, behind DU.

Gerry said he was ready for that. They probably wouldn't have been able to buy the boat anyway. Or they would have ended up with one of those commandeered boats that the Navy had covered with eight coats of grey paint. They would have been too old to sail the thing by the time they got the paint scraped off. It made more sense to get back in school right away. And he got to thinking about getting a car. He'd never had one. Now he really needed one. And he wanted a really nice one. He'd always imagined what it would be like to drive up to Mac's house, for instance, in a brand-new Cadillac. But when he walked into Rickenbaugh Cadillac with the twenty-two hundred-dollar bills in his hand, enough cash to buy the first 1946 Cadillac, the salesman just laughed at him. He said, "Son, do you have any idea how many customers, old, regular customers are on my list waiting for the first one to roll off the assembly line? It's going to take two years to fill the orders!" Gerry ended up buying a 1938 Oldsmobile with a Hydramatic transmission and slick tires.

It wasn't just his own when-the-war-is-over dreams that were crashing and burning; it was his parents' too. "The Folks" had plans for their son: Mom expected him to live right at home while he went to college. His younger brother, Dewey, was still in the Navy, so Gerry would have the room they had shared all to himself. He could save his money and invest it in Dad's construction business. He could even make a little extra money doing cleanup work for Dad. His father and older brother, Lafe, were building twenty houses just west of Colorado Boulevard. They'd already sold half of them by the time they'd poured the foundations. Times had never been better. There was a housing boom. The GI mortgages with 3 percent interest meant that practically any employed veteran who wanted to could buy a little house of his own—the American Dream—though not necessarily everyone's dream.

1946 Basic Training

Gerry knew what most young males knew about sex. Instead of spending three years preparing to live as an adult in a reasonable world, he spent them learning to be a warrior in the second war to end all wars. He didn't know anything at all about women. Of course, he knew all the jokes and clichés. His mother had given him plenty of warnings. Even good girls were bad. They got themselves "in trouble" to catch a man. He didn't really believe George about the teeth in their vaginas. That was absurd, but somehow he could never quite get that image out of his mind. Then there were the VD movies. The Navy showed terrifying films and gave lectures about syphilis and gonorrhea, chancres, puss, and retarded babies with saber shins. Rubbers were supposed to help prevent venereal disease, but George told him they ruined sex. There was a new drug called penicillin that could cure syphilis if you knew you had it, but the Navy recommended staying away from women altogether. If they weren't diseased, they wanted to marry you, especially if you were an officer, just to get your Navy pay. Or collect your insurance. He was not going to fall for any of that.

Gerry and his friend Bob Thompson, new Navy enlistees, 1942

Because I had lived almost exclusively in a female world, I knew very little about men. Even in my foster home I had little contact with Mr. Wood. I was not allowed to get up in the morning until he had eaten his breakfast and gone to work. In the evening, if he got home before dinner, I was not to bother him until he had finished reading the Evening *Herald Express*. On Saturdays, he usually spent most of the day working on his automobile or occasionally on the "company car," the one he drove all day for the telephone company. He wasn't aloof. Most of the time he was just a figure in a suit who smelled like cigarette smoke, but I knew from the deference Mrs. Wood showed him that he was more important than the rest of the household. Even the clothes in the closet they shared bespoke his greater worth. Mrs. Wood's portion had a few rayon print dresses that she wore to church and a cotton housedress or two and a coat. She had a red fox fur piece that bit its own tail, but I never saw her wear it. His part of the closet had six, maybe seven three-piece suits. The closet shelf above them contained two hatboxes full of Mrs. Wood's Sunday hats and a row of Mr. Wood's Stetson hats, several felt fedoras, a panama fedora, two straw boaters, and a cap. The shoe bag on the door held perhaps six pairs of his polished Florsheim shoes.

I liked Billy Wood on Saturdays. He was "Daddy" then, usually working on his car. The first car was an Essex, then he got a Chevy. It was streamlined. The last car he had was a Studebaker President. On Sundays he drove me to Sunday School and went back home to pick up Mrs. Wood. Maybe that was when they did their routine wild thing. Maybe that is the real reason that he never seemed to mind driving me to Sunday School.

One time, the only time I remember being home alone with him, when Mother Wood was downtown shopping, I was surprised and happy when Daddy became quite playful, chasing me around, and the two of us had laughed. It had never happened before. When he caught me, he kissed me, picked me up, and carried me into their bedroom. He put me down on the bed, then suddenly turned and left the room, saying, "Get up." And "Don't tell Mother about this." I was puzzled. I knew something was wrong, but it was a long time before I understood what it was.

Another time, he chastised me when I was thirteen or so and we were vacationing in Crestline. I had gone fishing for sun perch and met a boy my own age who liked fishing as much as I did. We had just noticed that the sun was low in the sky and started walking toward our rented cabins when we encountered Mr. Wood driving toward us. I think I was just embarrassed when he got out of the car and yelled at me. He had never hit me or even threatened to, but then he raised his hand to me, justifying it by saying I had a heart of stone. I remember being sent to one of the bedrooms and crying until I was dizzy. My hands were in tight fists that I couldn't open. I wasn't hitting anything with them, I just couldn't get them to open.

I had the usual mixture of ignorance and misinformation about sex that one accumulates in a home where the word sex is never uttered. Never. DeLoris had taught me most of what I knew about sex, but even she didn't use the word. The instruction was quite informal and sporadic at best. I would hear a word at school and ask her what it meant. The day I brought home F-U-C-K she got angry and said I would bring home the very worst word there was, but she didn't tell me its meaning and I couldn't find it in the dictionary. It was apparently a very rare word. Before I took life science at Horace Mann Junior High School I knew no words for

MARJORIE MAY'S 12th BIRTHDAY

•

By Mary Pauline Callender

MOTHERS! DON'T WAIT!

REMEMBERING the heartaches and embarrassed hours of YOUR "Twelfth Birthday", can you wait another day before enlightening your child?

There isn't one mother in a thousand whose gift of eloquence enables her to advise her daughter of the coming of menstruation, but Mary Pauline Callender tells the story in so simple and motherly a manner that your child unconsciously gives the credit to YOU for the enlightenment.

Following these simple rules will set your mind at peace:

1. Buy a Box of Kotex sanitary napkins also a Kotex Narrow Adjustable Belt.
2. Place the Marjorie May Booklet in, or on the top of, the wrapped package.
3. Lay the package on your daughter's bed or on her dresser.
4. Be sure and arrange all this so the child will be *alone* and undisturbed while she reads the story. With the keen perception of her age, she will immediately know that mother has again proved to be her best friend.

By following this plan, your burden is turned into a blessing. In after years when your child has grown into womanhood and others tell her of a heartbreaking first menstrual e x p e r i e n c e YOUR daughter will proudly say, "My Mother was different. She instructed me well in advance and I shall do the same with my children."

Pamphlet like the one DeLoris ordered for me

my own mysterious body parts. They were collectively referred to as "down there." In ninth grade life science I learned some actual anatomical terms, like pistil and stamen. Pollen. I think the Manhattan Project—the program that created the atom bomb using physicists who worked separately and secretly on their particular piece of the puzzle so that they couldn't know what they were doing collectively—must have been guarded by the same security system.

Had DeLoris not warned me when I was eleven that I was going to "get the cramps" and "come sick," and shown me the big blue box in the closet and the copy of *Marjorie May's Twelfth Birthday,* she had ordered through the mail for me, I would have had no idea at all what was happening the summer I started menstruating. Mother Wood was so very disappointed we were away from home and the supplies she had bought me. I would just have to do what she used to do in the old days, use a rag and wash it out in the basin. She followed the pinning of the rag to a pair of clean underpants with warnings about the consequences of taking baths during one's "sick time." Fortunately, there was no bathtub in the cabin, so I at least avoided the cryptic hazards of water.

For all the hubbub, I still had no clue at all about what was going on in my body. No one explained it. The inconvenient bleeding was just another of life's many mysteries. I would have to take another look at *Marjorie May's Twelfth Birthday.*

Of course, my sex education was not limited to menstruation and pollination. I had also read a library book by Zane Grey, *Riders of the Purple Sage,* I think it was. I just remember the author mentioning bare breasts. I think Helen Hunt Jackson's *Ramona* also had them or, being a Christian romance, maybe she had a bosom instead of breasts and just heaved. In Colorado, my friends talked a good bit about sex, mainly jokes that I rarely understood. I never heard anything at all about their own activities, if any. In eleventh grade, while visiting Cynthia Anderson's mountain home, I'd even paged through an illustrated copy of the *Kama Sutra.* I think her physician dad left it out for his four daughters to discover and share with their friends. It was interesting but had none of the information that I was seeking. It seemed to me to be about contortionists, not ordinary people. Today, I downloaded a free copy onto my iPad. Regrettably, the free copy has no illustrations. I haven't read it all yet, but

as far as I can tell it's just an overblown manual for making use of those troublesome four-hour erections which we so often see advertised on television these days.

In these days of overexposure to belly flab and buttocks cleavage, I sometimes wish more people of all sexes and inclinations in the United States wore burkas. But I never wish to return to the days of my youth, when the human body itself was considered a crime against nature. From 1930 to 1968 the Hays Office defined and enforced film-able human behavior through the Motion Picture Production Code. Married couples always slept in twin beds and their mouths were hermetically sealed. There were no onscreen erotic kisses until 1944, when Alfred Hitchcock made *Lifeboat* with Tallulah Bankhead. A real "French" kiss wouldn't be seen until

Natalie Wood's and Warren Beatty's in *Splendor in the Grass.* In 1961 Ingrid Bergman's Swedish films were banned for seven years in the United States, after she, a married woman, had a scandalous affair with the director, Roberto Rossellini, while making the film, *Stromboli* (released in 1950).

In 1975 I attended the thirtieth reunion of my East Denver High School class. Just mentioning the names of two girls known to be sexually active in high school brought the house down. Nice girls, girls destined to be ladies, allegedly remained virgins until that wild and transcendent moment that followed an extravagant ceremony at St. John's Cathedral, or a more modest one in the chapel, the truly important thing being that she vow to love, honor, and obey him until the day he or she dearly departed.

After the ceremony, the dewy-eyed couple would become one person, that person being bride + groom = bridegroom. In celebration of the melding, the virtual loss of her legal identity and actual loss of both her name and free will, her parents would invite several hundred of their closest friends, some of whom they had never met, to a feast at the Denver Country Club, where the newly melded One would simultaneously feed its two mouths wedding cake. Soon after the conspicuous consumption, the Oneness would be driven off to its undisclosed destination (even without disclosure, everyone knew it was the Bridal Suite at the Broadmoor) in a Lincoln Continental convertible with tin cans rattling behind it. Then, trembling with anticipation, the nice girl, stripped of any and all responsibility, was finally free to do whatever he pleased.

So, I realized I was an ordinary slut when, on our engagement night, I gave into my own ever-more-demanding baser instincts, of my own free will—but for him. I had heard somewhere of the unspeakable pain men endured when aroused by some low-life prick-tease who did not follow through. That was just the fine print I was looking for to preserve a modicum of decency. I loved him far too much to torture him that way.

A CODE
TO GOVERN THE MAKING
OF MOTION AND TALKING
PICTURES

the

Reasons Supporting It

And the

Resolutions for Uniform

Interpretation

by

Motion Picture Producers and Distributors of America, Inc.

JUNE 11 1934

1946 ENGAGEMENT

I had read Philip Wylie's *Generation of Vipers* the year before I met Gerry
so was pretty well steeped in the evils of Momism. I was looking for it, but
it did seem to me that Gerry's "Mom" had come through the war
unscathed and still in charge. Mrs. McClard was responsible for Gerry's
bad haircut. She had also thought that replacing the brass buttons on his
blues would transform them to mufti. The French-toed shoes and
Homburg hat that he wore the evening he picked me up to go to dinner at
his parents' house were his own idea. He probably hoped his mom would
like me. He said, "She and Dad are really looking forward to meeting you.
Mom even made a special supper."

On the way, Gerry explained that his parents were from Arkansas and
they ate dinner, their biggest meal, at noon. Tonight, however, she was
serving four thick porterhouse steaks he'd bought her because he wanted
his family to share what he'd gotten to eat at the officer's club. He couldn't
wait to see his parents take their first bite of a really good steak. Mrs.
McClard, like Mrs. Wood, had never eaten anything but chicken fried
round steak that had been pounded and dipped in flour, then fried in
bacon fat or lard and cooked until it was well done. Gerry was surprised to

Mr. and Mrs. McClard with one of their offspring, date unknown

Gerry with Mr. and Mrs. McClard

see that his mother had prepared the porterhouse the same way, then smothered it in cream gravy. There were butter beans cooked with ham. Ordinarily, had she not been showing off, she would have made a batch of golden-crusted cornbread as she did every day. Instead, probably as a treat, she had stacked Wonder Bread on a china salad plate that also served as an ashtray for Mr. McClard's lighted cigarette.

His parents agreed that the steak hadn't "fried up as good as a nice big round steak." They thought maybe next time he should get it cut thinner.

I don't remember dessert; I only remember that Mr. McClard ended the meal by tearing pieces of the bread into a tumbler of milk and eating it with a spoon.

I had grown up eating variations of that meal, minus the porterhouse, in the Wood's household. I didn't quite understand all that it implied. I thought it was a sign, something like "Leaving Colorful Colorado." It should have said "Absolutely No Trespassing—Guard Dogs on Duty." Had Gerry's mother not taken an immediate and permanent dislike to me we might have become friends eventually. Probably not. I was pretty insecure about my own place in the world, not to mention superficial. Because of my own family, I was very class conscious, and eager to be distinguished from people I viewed as socially inferior.

Gerry had hesitated to tell his mother about the engagement, because...well.... We were halfway through dinner at the McClards' when she spotted it. She said it sure was a pretty ring. I must have beamed at Gerry as I said, "I think so too," and he must have said that we were planning to get married. Gerry had not mentioned our intentions (but maybe, deep down, they weren't actually his intentions). He said he'd wanted to surprise her, but I know he was afraid to tell her. What I didn't understand at all was that he also must have been feeling some ambivalence, at the very least.

I was more than ambivalent myself, and some of my own negative feelings sprang directly from how I knew "my people" would perceive the McClards. They were what Mother would consider crude and ignorant, and call "very ordinary." Associating myself with them would endanger my place in the McKenzie family right as I was at the height of my sense of belonging. Not only had I been vetted by national alums and then invited to become a charter member of Delta Gamma at DU, even better, I had been rushed and then pledged as a Pi Beta Phi at DU. This was quite an accomplishment in the family. Mr. McKenzie's sister, Isabel, had been the president of the CU charter chapter in her day, and it was therefore assumed that the twins would get in as legacies but they had instead been humiliated by being snubbed, due to the questionable morals of their—our—mother. Everybody in the family was so proud of me for that triumph. The idea of losing the glory of belonging seemed at the time every bit as intolerable as that of giving up my artistic ambition of being a writer. Sure enough, when my mother found out I was engaged she said, "To him?"

*   *   *

Less than a month later, I was throwing up in the toilet of my mother's apartment, suspecting it was a sign of pregnancy. Perhaps before I suspected it I had mentioned this recent ailment to Gerry—which may explain why he suddenly loaded his car on the other side of town a day or two before his birthday, our proposed wedding day, preparing to take off on the wedding trip we had planned, had drawn on gas station maps with grease pencil.

We were going to go to Yellowstone, by way of the Grand Tetons. I had always wanted to see Old Faithful. He wanted to see everything: the Morning Glory Pool, the Paint Pots, steaming springs. He wanted to see a herd of bison take over a road, elk and moose—and bears so brazen that they walked right up to the car. He said we'd really have to be careful where we pitched our tent. "A bear won't bother getting through the flap; it'll just rip one side open, walk in, rip the other, and walk out. He'd always wanted to go to Glacier National Park and Banff. He said we would stop in Seattle, maybe go to the Olympic Peninsula. We both wanted to see the Hoh Rainforest. We had planned to spend a day or two in San Francisco and then meander down the coast, through Santa Cruz, Monterey....

But he was not going with me. He was going with Charles Davies, a nasty, prancing young man with a sardonic smile. Gerry's flight made sense, even at the time. All of his dreams had been smothered by my thin body, devoured, turned into a pulsating glob of flesh. We both felt trapped; the only difference was that he could run away—or thought he could. I had sensed it, that it was never to be a wedding trip, and, in fairness, had I not also sensed that I was pregnant, I would not have been at all sorry. I would have welcomed the chance to back out. Still, my sadness and fury at his months-long disappearance can well up painfully to this day.

When I went to the McClards' a few days later to ask about Gerry, Mrs. McClard slammed the door in my face. That was when I started to hate her and when I started to think of myself as on my own. I thought my options were to get an illegal abortion, give the baby up for adoption, or try to raise it by myself. Mother was frantic, kind to me, but completely unable to cope. One day, she would say something like, "We could go to

Gerald 1946

Gerry on the "honeymoon" trip that he took with Charles Davies instead of me

Southern England. I think Chaunce was making *The Scarlet Pimpernel* there." (Chaunce had worked on the film in England very briefly in 1934. He was fired.) Another time she thought we should move to Mexico City. She had heard Chaunce was working on something there.

I don't know at what point Mother decided to look up an old friend of her late husband, an attorney who suggested the suit. I can't even remember the time, but maybe when I was around four-months pregnant we went to court, where Gerry and I were both humiliated and degraded. Mr. McClard laughed at my assertion that I was a virgin when I met Gerry. Gerry claimed I was a seductress. He described the black dress I had worn on the night we got engaged, a dress that suggested to him that I was more than available. The judge clearly disdained Gerry and ruled that he would be held financially responsible for my medical expenses and the baby.

When I was five months pregnant, I heard Gerry's great stride taking the stairs two at a time. I hadn't seen him in more than four months except in the courtroom. I had assumed I would never see him again.

He wanted to see me, just talk with me. He loved me, he said. He loved his baby. He wanted to marry me. I said that we could get married so the baby would not be a bastard and then we could get a divorce. He said that he didn't want it that way, that he wanted to marry me forever, take care of me...and his baby.

The next day, a Saturday, we drove to Cheyenne, Wyoming, dressed in our best clothes; he in his vested, tailor-made suit, with the extra pair of pants carefully folded on the back seat, I in my fashionable calf-length suit, which almost concealed my five-month pregnancy. He vowed to love and to cherish me. I vowed, silently, to stay with him until he finished school. I vowed to support his dream. I fantasized giving up nothing at all.

* * *

I think Gerry was able to make this decision to get married and act on it only because Mrs. McClard was away in California, visiting her sister. In I.V. McClard's mind, the worst thing that could have happened to her son in the course of the war would have been getting mixed up with some woman. He had never had a girlfriend before he went into the service— unless you counted the dentist's daughter, Gilberta Lininger. Gerry always described Gilberta as "really sweet." Gerry and Gilberta were about the same age, but they went to different schools. He went to South High and she went to Boettcher School for Crippled Children. Her legs had been stunted and twisted by osteomyelitis when she was a child. Gerry said she had a great sense of humor. She was almost like a sister. Tenderness is tenderness, and as a young boy, he might not have been able to distinguish compassion from love. They both loved to go to movies and sometimes Mom went along too. He liked her a lot, but he couldn't help feeling sorry for her. He knew that Gilberta saw their relationship in a different light. She had written him V-mail letters when he was in the Navy and he responded to them until the number of X's and O's began running off the page and she began mentioning her hope chest.

It was toward the end of the war, while he was in Jacksonville preparing for another tour of duty in the South Pacific, when he first had a serious relationship with a woman. He claimed she was "an older woman." Apparently, she taught him everything he knew about lovemaking. (It wasn't near enough.) Then, suddenly, the war was over and he was home. Maybe the war ended before the relationship did, and maybe everything got mixed up and I sat down at the wrong table. Maybe that's why, right after Michael was born, Mrs. McClard started forwarding the mail from Jacksonville, Florida. I only remember the first postcard. She must have had it made on an amusement pier, just for him. It had a photograph of the sender, not looking especially old, just experienced. She was posing provocatively on top of a white baby grand piano.

I doubt the McClards preferred the woman from Jacksonville to me, but Mom wanted to make sure I knew they didn't like *me*. Because I.V. didn't like me from day one, I knew it was more than that I was pregnant. Yes, I did fulfill their idea of the seductive entrapper, but maybe they also thought I was putting on airs, was a snob, looking down on them, because of course, stupidly, I was. Before we ever knew we were to have our own war the battle lines had been drawn.

1947 MICHAEL AND FARRAGUT

I don't plan to detail the seventeen years of marriage that resulted from my being late to register for school and Gerry's having bought his zoology book too soon. Our early marriage had its moments: Topping those moments for me was having a healthy baby boy and deciding after my very careful inspection that he was normal. At least he seemed to be.

I was not normal though. My breast milk didn't look anything like golden Guernsey. It was watery, blue looking. I put Michael on formula right away. I followed the directions exactly, measured everything with the same care I had used in my chemistry class at East, but I always came out an ounce short in the last bottle. I cried. I was not fit to be a mother, and my husband was not going to be a doctor as I had thought.

We were flat broke, with no place to go. We knew we had made a big mistake, ruined both of our dreams of becoming who we wanted to be. We got in that Oldsmobile and then again ran away to California. Maybe Auntie could help. Also, George was there, living with his parents. Auntie only had one bedroom, though, so there was no room for us. She did want to help. We stayed briefly with some of her neighbors in a nice attic room. When we were leaving, I was embarrassed to notice that Gerry had put a

Farragut Technical College and Institute, Museum of North Idaho, from the 1948 Stag Yearbook.

cigarette down and burned some of their nice furniture. We lived with another friend of Auntie's when Michael was born. Finally, we were able to rent a space in a squalid temporary project built for WWII workers.

It seemed for a few months that Gerry would be a person who worked graveyard shift at Shell Chemical, walking on a catwalk above vats of N-butyldiamine, a nasty smelling, carcinogenic chemical. He slept all day and worked all night. On Saturday's, Gerry and George worked on their cars while I stayed with our baby in our horrible little apartment. Except for Michael's birth, San Pedro was a dark and frightening time, and the whole year is mostly a hole in my mind.

Not that I was sad; I just felt that I had lost my freedom. I remember being lonely, cutoff, something akin to being in a minimum-security prison. I had no control of my life. When he was a resident at the Naval Hospital in Philadelphia, I described that phase of my life to my dear (and only) friend, Page Stickney, as being in a cocoon. At other times, it felt more like a shroud.

* * *

Just when life began to look like Mrs. McClard had said it would, Mac told Gerry about an article he had read in *Liberty* magazine about the new college in Idaho that had opened on an old Navy base. It was designed especially for veterans. If he went there, he would not have to go back to Colorado with his wife and new baby and try to explain it all to his mom.

Before you could say "butyldiamine," we were on our way to Farragut, Idaho, from San Pedro, California, in our 1938 Oldsmobile that was burning oil even before the trailer was hooked up.

Our beautiful baby boy slept, well...like a baby, in his blue bassinet on the backseat of the car. Gerry had fifty dollars in the pocket of the trousers that had once been part of one of his naval aviator's uniforms. We got all the way to the south shore of the Columbia River before we had to stop and camp overnight, waiting for my mother to wire us enough money to pay for a rebuilt carburetor.

Farragut Navy Base was briefly transformed into Farragut College and Technical Institute, and is now Farragut State Park. "Our Utopia is nothing but a goddamned Navy base," were Gerry's first words when we arrived, but it was so much more than that. Located on the southern tip of Lake Pend Oreille in the Coeur d'Alene Mountains, themselves in the Idaho panhandle, it was an abandoned naval base in the middle of a little natural paradise. The most lovely thing about being there, though, turned out to be that Gerry and I had a chance to be a family with Michael without the influence of anyone who wished either of us or our families any ill.

We found many things we had in common. We loved fishing together for landlocked kokanee along the shores of Lake Pend Oreille, bringing them home, scraping off their silver scales, cooking them on our wood stove, and eating their delicate salmon flesh. We dreamt, but never even caught a glimpse, of a Kamloops, the giant rainbow trout that usually swam two hundred feet below the surface, where it too, thrived on kokanee. As we hiked and fished we talked of many things, and laughed together. We relished each other's company.

One spring morning we rose early to hike up gentle slopes, with no trails, just soft turf dotted with a few flowers. Gerry alternately carried Michael like an emperor on his shoulders or under one arm like a sack of flour. We prowled around two sagging log houses, built by settlers so long ago that the daffodils planted there had gone back to being the wild narcissi of their ancient beginnings. I couldn't help wondering about the women who had carried them there as treasured bulbs dug from their gardens in the East. But there were other gardeners at work that I didn't know about at all. It was the first place I saw trillium, pristine and white. I didn't know then that ants carry their seeds from forest to meadow as they forage in the humus below the land we claim to own. My mother had remembered painted trillium growing in her native Nebraska. I like to think that her mother remembered it growing in her native North Carolina, as I, a carrier of memories, remember it now.

I don't know whether it was that morning or some other that we stood in silence, watching a mule deer approach a split-rail fence, then more float than leap across and bound away into the haze.

In the fall, during doe season, I worried when Gerry went hunting. He had his old single shot rifle. He brought back a doe, no trophy, no musky meat that had to be disguised under sauce. We shared the venison with friends and neighbors and enjoyed the stews and roasts into the winter.

We were pilgrims, together, in the Promised Land.

We had good friends at Farragut. Our closest friends, Rose and Dick McMenemy, were also struggling through their first year of marriage and we shared many of the same prejudices about nearly everything from cooking to politics, although their opinions were generally better informed than ours. The McMenemys were in their mid-thirties. When they came to Farragut, Rose had left behind her independent life in St. Paul, where she had been a well-paid secretary for Northwest Airlines. She told me she cried a lot at first because she missed her old friends, especially her closest friend, Imelda. But then Rose said she had decided it was foolish to grieve over the loss of "a bunch of other old maids" when she had such a wonderful husband. Dick had also been unmarried before his marriage to Rose. He had worked for Northern Pacific Railroad his whole career, excepting his brief service in the army, but even his service was with the railroad. He had been one of the experienced workers drafted to rebuild and extend India's defunct railroad, an eight-hundred-mile link in the only supply line to our Chinese allies.

I don't remember how the McMenemys met, just Rose's story of their trip to Farragut. Because of Dick's history with the Northern Pacific Railroad, the couple rode as guests on the new streamliner, the North Coast Limited, from St. Paul to Spokane. The two of them were standing single file in line, waiting to get into the dining car, when Rose reached back to take her husband's hand. She just caught a ring finger and was surprised and a little worried that it felt so thin; the joints felt swollen. It crossed her mind that it might be a recurrence of arthritis from the malaria he'd contracted in India. She wondered if it hurt. Perhaps he should see a doctor when they arrived in Spokane. She said, "Your finger feels like a dried-up chicken neck." He didn't laugh. He yanked his finger loose. When she turned around, she discovered the finger she had clutched belonged to an elderly man to whom Dick had yielded his place in line.

One of the things I admired was their knack for making the best of things. They had turned their ward into a comfortable and inviting living space. Ours still looked like a storage room. I tried to emulate Rose's ability to transform ordinary food from the abandoned and restocked

Navy commissary into a feast using a hotplate and Sears Roebuck roaster oven. She gave me a worn copy of *The Joy of Cooking* (always just calling it "Irma": "Irma says...."). From Irma I learned to make venison stew and to prepare our kokanee "silvers." The McMenemys didn't fish, so we caught them, and Irma and Rose kept me from ruining them. But I never got much beyond that level as a cook.

Easter week, Rose demonstrated a technique for blowing the raw egg out of its shell to make Ukrainian eggs. She then demonstrated how to apply wax with a little brass "kistka" as she told us a little about the symbolism. We tried our hands at drawing and dying, but I only remember the crossed lines and the triangles and my puzzling about circles within circles representing the androgynous nature of God. We didn't blow our eggs, just boiled them, decorated them, and marveled at the emerging rich colors. Then, after spending hours creating our pagan, if not, blasphemous versions, we ate them, the ugliest first. In the many sessions of dying Easter eggs that followed during the years with my children, we always made at least a few with a faint Ukrainian heritage.

Our little sojourn in Paradise was so short. Enrollment in 1948 at Farragut College and Technical Institute was plummeting and they decided to close by the following year. We were forced to move on, to say goodbye, not just to our friends but to a time and place. I realize now how much we lost when we left Farragut, where we were on our own, not tied to our past. We had mutual friends and experiences and time to consider where we were, not just where we were going. Neither of us had to feel either left out or belittled in a world we had built from scratch. Looking back, I think we had the beginnings of a good marriage.

1948 Leaving Farragut

Nineteen forty-eight started out rather badly. I missed my period.

I felt it was largely my fault. We knew of three forms of birth control: condoms, diaphragms, and the rhythm method. Gerry didn't like condoms, we never had quite enough money for the initial fitting and purchase of a diaphragm, and I was completely unsuccessful at keeping track of ovulation. I don't remember having written anything on a calendar or even having a calendar, so I'm pretty sure I relied entirely on my own memory. I don't remember when I broke the news to Gerry, or when he came home with his own news: Farragut College was broke and closing at the end of the semester.

All of those nice professors who had come west to teach returning veterans (and possibly to get in a little fishing) were now scurrying around trying to find paying jobs. One of Gerry's professors, a borrowed Jesuit from Gonzaga University in nearby Spokane, urged Gerry to considered Gonzaga, mentioning that Bing Crosby was an alumnus. It wouldn't have been a bad choice academically, had we been able to get by in the city on the married student ninety-dollar-a-month stipend. But we had moved from our original housing in married officer's quarters because we couldn't

Gerry and me with newborn, Michael, 1947

afford the cord of wood we needed to keep our furnace, kitchen stove, and water heater going. (We were also tired of getting up in the middle of the night to stoke the furnace.) We barely squeaked by at Farragut, even in the converted isolation ward we moved into that included electric lights and steam heat for twenty-five dollars a month. But then neither of us had either experience or instruction in managing money.

Just after a physician in Coeur d'Alene had confirmed my pregnancy, I noticed that the curly-headed four-year-old twins who had come to Michael's first birthday party had a combination of tiny blisters and scabs on their faces and arms. I asked their mother what had happened to them. She smiled and said that it was nothing, just chickenpox, and she was glad to get it over with before they started to school. They hadn't been the least bit sick. She had called her doctor, who said they weren't contagious once they scabbed over. It wasn't long before every child in the area, including Michael, had chickenpox. Michael had five or six little pox and only a slight fever, so I didn't mind his "getting them out of the way," but I was pretty sure that I hadn't had chickenpox as a child. Mrs. Wood would have mentioned it. I knew that I'd had both measles and whooping cough. I just couldn't remember.

I certainly do remember *now* if and when I had varicella, a.k.a. chickenpox. It was February 1948. I was covered with itching vesicles, from a quarter to a half inch apart, as though I'd been rolling around in a patch of poison ivy. I lay on my hands through sleepless nights trying not to scratch. I had a fever and headache and still have a few scars from pox. When Mother saw me later that year, she was certain that I had actually had a mild case of smallpox. I will probably always wonder if the commonplace and seemingly benign varicella-zoster virus that not only causes children to have pneumonia and encephalitis but lingers for a lifetime at a nerve root to emerge as shingles (zoster), might not have damaged a two-month-old fetus.

That spring, after hearing that Farragut was about to fail, Gerry's father, Bert, sent him a letter that began "Dear Son." It said that he and I.V. actually *did* want to see their grandson. They had studied the snapshots Gerry sent them. They thought Michael was pretty but he needed a haircut and he looked a little peaked. Mr. McClard thought Gerry should return to Denver and reenroll at DU. George had dropped by and was enjoying being in college. He was planning to be an accountant. Gerry's dad said that he and "Miggins" could live in one of the units McClard & Son had finished in their four-unit court at Clarkson and Bayaud, until the project went on the market. Our unit would be right next door to Mom and Dad. Gerald could work for him in the summer. By then we could get a Quonset hut behind DU.

I dreaded returning to Denver and the McClards almost as much as I hated leaving our little utopian Farragut. At least we had the baby to look forward to and something that was almost as wonderful. We had a goal and we were pointed in the right direction. No matter what kind of difficulty we encountered, we would always know it was momentary. Ahead of us was that glorious day that Gerry would become a doctor. Not

Rose McMenemy with her daughter, born the year after we left Farragut

only would he become a doctor, he would become someone else entirely. A medical education would do for him what the Navy had claimed to do when it told him he was, in fact "an officer and a gentleman." As I would years later be told by Chet Goodfellow, my coworker in the art department of the Air Force Finance Center in Denver, I too would gain stature when Gerry was a doctor. Chet said he couldn't understand why I was so upset about losing my job because of being pregnant with Kevin, our third child. "Three months from now, Gerry will graduate from medical school, and you will be a doctor's wife. Then everyone will respect you."

On the other hand, had we stayed away from Denver and built our lives and ourselves from the ground up, we might still be married. Instead, Gerry ended up largely controlled by his family and I, in turn, was controlled by Gerry's expectations and parent-guided tastes and unilateral choices.

1948 John Christopher

As soon as we got back to Denver, I made an appointment with Dr. Cyrus
W. Anderson, the father of my best friend in high school, Cynthia. He was
a family doctor who had patented a slide rule for determining the precise
moment that the egg of the month would fall free to land in a throng of
sperm, a tiny iteration of the Times Square countdown on New Year's
Eve. I had spent quite a bit of time, probably too much, at the Anderson's
mountain cabin in the summer of '45, when I was working as a waitress at
Woodbine Lodge in Jarre Canyon. I felt comfortable with the family.
Dr. Anderson only left his practice on Wednesdays to join the family at the
cabin. I didn't know him except by his deeds: He had dammed a tiny
trickle of a creek to create Papoose Lake, a large pond for his family to
swim in, and secured a rope to a tall, stout tree for swimmers to swing out
from shore and splash down in deeper water. He had made a clay tennis
court where his daughters learned to tolerate visitors like me who winced
or ducked when the ball came within range. And once, as my friend
Cynthia and I cowered in our beds, Dr. Anderson, groggy, but competent,
grabbed a shirt from its hook on Cynthia's bedroom door to protect his

Left: Lake Pend Oreille, courtesy of Museum of North Idaho

hand as he scrunched a poor, harmless brown bat whose only mistake had
been seeking shelter in the wrong room.

He was the hero father of what seemed to me to be the model family
and naturally, as such a paragon, he was president of Rotary Club and
Mercy Hospital. After my first visit to his office he mentioned that he
needed five hundred Christmas cards: four hundred linoleum block prints
for Rotary and one hundred simple watercolors of carolers for his hospital
staff. I'm not sure how he knew I made Christmas cards, but he asked me
if I would care to make his. By an odd coincidence, the hundred and fifty
dollars I would get for doing the cards would pay for the baby's delivery
and leave a little money for presents for Michael. Everything was working
out!

We settled in for the summer in the promised one-bedroom
apartment. As soon as Gerry got his first paycheck, we bought a really
awful, limed oak table, chairs, and buffet. I picked it out myself. (I hate to
think that it might still be out there somewhere making some woman wish
she had just kept her rickety old Samsonite bridge table instead.) The
dining-room furniture, along with the soiled sectional Cynthia gave us, got
us all the way through medical school and Gerry's residency. In fact, the
sectional, reupholstered, lasted until the Bekins Moving Company
auctioned it off along with the rest of our things when I was in my final
year of graduate school. Who knew that a mistaken purchase would follow
a family to the ends of the earth, like an immortal but mangy dog running
after its master's car?

The baby was due in early September. I had hoped he would be born
on my birthday but he was overdue. After a week of waiting, Dr. Anderson
decided that if the baby didn't come by the following weekend he would
have to induce me, because he was going out of town. In 1948, "inducing"
usually meant giving the mother a dose of castor oil. If that didn't work she
was usually given Pitocin, a synthetic oxytocin that tricks the uterus into
contracting. In my case, September 18, 1948 I had my dose of castor oil and
orange juice in the morning. Later in the day, I was given Pitocin and Dr.
Anderson told the head nurse, a Sister of Mercy, to call him as soon I was
three fingers dilated. Before she went off duty at eleven, I heard her
instructing the on-duty nurse to call Dr. Anderson, because I was ready.
The new nurse checked me and decided Sister Mary Whatever had been

wrong. A very short time later, when I began to have bearing-down pains, I turned on my light to summon her. The group of nurses talking and laughing right outside of my door continued to do so. I called out to them. Finally one of them came in, examined me, sent for a gurney, and wheeled me into a room where one nurse stood at the head of the gurney and slopped ether from a can over a gauze mask, while another stood at my feet, holding my legs together, and telling me to breathe.

Doctor Anderson got there just in time to deliver the baby. When I saw the doctor in the morning, he said I had a healthy boy and that everything was working. "He peed on me right away!"

The first time I got him in my grasp, I unwrapped him to inspect him, and marveled, as all new mothers must, at the perfection of his hands with its tiny nails, his pretty head—bald, as his brother's had been—and touched his "soft spot," the frontal fontanel, that allows the newborn to be forced into the world through the birth canal, but makes him seem so vulnerable. When he opened his eyes seeming to look at me, I thought they were a lighter grey than Michael's dark eyes had been at birth. I was sure he was going to have blue eyes like Gerry's.

We named him John Christopher. His first two days, a nurse brought him in for all of his feedings and I nursed him, worrying, hoping that when my milk came in, it would be both rich and plentiful. I imagined the brothers, playing together, growing up. As I had with Michael, I thought of war and, "Now I am become death, the destroyer of worlds" and the terrible hydrogen bomb, so much more powerful than those that ended the war, and how our former allies had become our enemies.

A high school friend sent a blue challis kimono. It was lined with sheer white silk and embroidered at the neck with French knots and tiny flowers. I thought I would dress him in it when we took him home.

Mardie left roses from her garden at the nurses' station.

The next day, September 21, was the last day of summer. At six in the morning, I could hear the babies crying in the hall and readied myself for John Christopher's arrival, but the starched nurse didn't bring him. I decided he was probably being circumcised. When Dr. Anderson came in, he said the baby was fine, but that he'd had a little blue spell. "Nothing to worry about—it happens all the time. Mucous. A little mucous in his windpipe." He said they'd sucked it right out, but he wanted to keep an eye on him. The nurse would be in to pump my breasts, then feed him in the nursery, that they would "probably bring him in to nurse at ten."

At ten, a nurse brought him to me, but before he had even begun to nurse, I noticed his fingernails were blue. I turned on the call light and beckoned to a passing nurse, who rushed in, looked at him and said that it was probably just more mucous, and took him away. Someone would be in to pump my breasts she said.

I looked at the roses Mardie had sent and thought that John Christopher would never see roses.

In time, another nurse arrived and managed to get a small amount of colostrum from my breasts before holding it up to the light and chiding, "Some nursing mother you are!" I don't think she meant to be unkind. She was just awkward and said an honest thing the wrong way.

When it was time for the two o'clock feeding, instead of a nurse in the door with a swaddled baby, it was Gerry, hesitating there, trying to say what he couldn't say. About a half an hour before, our baby, who had never heard his name, had died of a massive hemorrhage in his lungs. The pediatrician called by Dr. Anderson was present but could not have saved him. Had it been possible, in 1948, few doctors would have chosen to rescue a baby whose brain had been repeatedly deprived of oxygen.

We never really knew what caused the hemorrhage. The pathology report that I received two weeks later said it was hemorrhagic disease of the newborn, a condition resulting from a vitamin K deficiency, but I'm pretty sure he had been given the shot; it was part of the birthing routine. Furthermore, the description was not at all typical. The chief obstetrics resident who delivered my next baby, six years later, at Colorado General, said he was nearly certain his John Christopher's death was from damage due to the nurse's having held my legs together, but when I had mentioned the leg-holding to Dr. Anderson in 1948, he said, simply, "My girls don't do that," a statement that both made me feel as though I had been accused of lying, and made me wonder why he denied it had happened. The truth was, that until it happened to me, I had never even dreamed that there was a way to forestall a baby's birth. Much later, I wondered about the chickenpox I had early in my pregnancy. It is always remarkable how many hazards any baby has on its way into the world. Whatever went wrong, my interest was simply in knowing, not in placing blame.

Then as now, I understood that losing a newborn baby is a different thing entirely from losing an older child. And I knew that my mother was speaking the truth when she said that a newborn's death was barely a ripple, but I wish she hadn't said that. It strengthened my conviction that I didn't have a right to express, or possibly even acknowledge, my sorrow. My rational self, the part of me that does all the thinking and moralizing and tongue clicking, held that "Death was disappointing but life goes on. Grieving about such a small thing is self-indulgent. Be thankful for what you have. Don't cry around Michael; it will frighten him. He will think you hurt yourself."

I am not, by nature, rational. Just like my infant, I was born raw and primitive. I didn't know then, that underneath the thin proud flesh, I was just as raw as the day I was born. I thought September 7, 1948, when I turned twenty-one, was my personal cutoff date for childish ways. I thought adults were people who could deal with reality. Soon after John Christopher's momentary life, I began to say, "Who cares?" about anything of importance. Although it seemed to be a way of shrugging my shoulders, it might have been an actual question.

When Canon Watts visited me on the way to the little graveside service that I didn't attend, he knew, without hearing me ask; he said, just to me, "You know how much you love that baby? God loves him infinitely more." Some part of me still struggles to believe that but another part tells me that just opening his eyes was his entire life experience, and it was timeless. It was his moment.

1948 HOUSEWIFE'S DEPRESSION

As planned, in the fall, we moved into the little house on South Pierson Street with the extra bedroom, the black-and-tan terrier, the black widow spider under the sink, the baby rattlers out back, and the job that would pay the mortgage. It really had just about everything except a phone or any form of transportation besides the Oldsmobile and a little red wagon. We were about an hour away from central Denver. We didn't need Public Service electricity. The Rural Electrification Act supplied our electricity, and we didn't have to pay sewer taxes because we had our very own septic tank right there in the back yard. Of course, we had running water and we didn't have to pay the greedy City of Denver for it. The water for all of those little clapboard houses had to be hauled in a small tanker truck from a source inside the Rocky Mountain Arsenal and then pumped into a wooden water tower. There were even days that I felt grateful that Michael's baby brother wasn't lying in a bassinet in Michael's bedroom, hooked up to tubes, not knowing, just being.

That was Gerry's job: hauling the water and filling the reservoir once a week. It only took half of Saturday. Mr. McClard even paid George a little something to drive out and help Gerald with the water. At noon on

Michael, at about eighteen months, 1948

Saturday, the two Macs would come in, laughing about their morning mishaps, for lunch. Often, the rest of the day they spent working on the jacked-up Oldsmobile in front of the house. Both of them were pretty good mechanics. Once Gerry spent the entire weekend rebuilding the transmission by himself. He was so pleased, as he began to close the gearbox he called me out to see what he had done. Before I could get my hands dry from the dishes, I heard him say, "SHIT!" He had just spotted a small gear on the curb.

Except for lunch, my Saturday mornings were pretty much the same as every other morning. I was in the house, washing clothes that never looked as clean as I wanted them to look, or scrubbing floors that were never spotless like Marge's floors, or wiping bathroom walls that always seemed to be urine-splattered, or cleaning a carpet that I wished I had never bought, with a carpet-sweeper that always needed to be emptied into a trash can that was already full. I talked and played with my dear two-year-old son, who didn't eat as much as I thought he should and wasn't as fat as his cousin who was four months younger. Sometimes, in the afternoon, while he slept, I sewed clothes for him and wished I had a sewing machine.

Sometimes, I just let everything go, the dishes, the floors, and the splattered wall. That year I wrote and illustrated a children's book, *Id in Noo*, the first book I ever wrote hoping to publish. The story was about a tiny boy who lives under a mushroom and yearns to build a bridge to the moon, an ambition that seems to exceed his abilities. After numerous attempts to be what he is not, he finally succeeds when he falls asleep while trying to paint a patch of pale flowers. The paint he uses evaporates and forms a rainbow across the dome of the sky.

Writing the book was my way of grieving. When I was twenty-one, I had some cockeyed notion that beside the enormity of World War II, the loss of a three-day-old infant was not something to cry about, or even talk about. I didn't yet know that all loss is personal. I had never seen the *Pietà*.

Without knowing anything about the submission of either illustrations or manuscripts, when it was finished, I put the hand-lettered manuscript, the watercolor illustrations, the dedication to John Christopher, and a self-addressed, stamped envelope all into another envelope and sent it, airmail, to Harpers. It wasn't long before they sent it back with a note saying they really liked the illustrations. But it wasn't right for their house. I never sent it out again.

For Gerry, weekdays were different from Saturdays. He drove off in the Oldsmobile at seven in the morning so he'd be sure to get a parking place on Warren Avenue. Maybe he'd have time to stop by the student union for a cup of coffee before he went to class. Then he'd go to biochemistry or microbiology or introduction to philosophy or calculus. Wherever he went, he was on his way somewhere that I knew I could never go.

On the afternoons that he didn't have lab, as soon as his classes were over, he'd almost always stop by Mac's Quonset, where I imagined they sat around laughing and reminiscing about all the times they'd coasted down Ruby Hill in their wagons, or slid down on their inner tubes, or the day Gerry tried out the wings they had made and almost dislocated his shoulder when he jumped off the fence. Some days they probably talked about the time Gerry was in the mid-air collision over King Ranch and couldn't get the canopy open, or the time the Kamikaze hit the carrier right behind the one that George was on. Then something would remind Gerry that it was time to get home to dinner and his kid and sulky wife. He might remember to stop by the Safeway on Alameda and get some stuff. What had she said she needed? Oh well.

Weeknights, right after dinner, as soon as the dishes were cleared, while I was putting Michael to bed, Gerry would spread out his books and papers on the dining-room table under the one light good enough to read by. I probably did the dishes and left the pans to soak. I don't remember what I did. I only remember the feeling of not having done anything that wouldn't have to be done again tomorrow and tomorrow and tomorrow.

Weekend evenings were different. Friday nights we went to a movie, usually, if the weather was nice, to a drive-in. Michael would sleep in the back seat and I often dozed in the front. Gerry loved westerns. I liked a few. Saturdays we always went to see George and Marge, invited or not. The McCormicks often had other guests, Marge's friends from high school and her mother, Mrs. Wimberly, and occasionally, her brother, an alcoholic mailman. Usually the men sat on straight chairs at one side of the room while the women sat on the couch and matching chair on the other side. The women talked about their mutual friends, their babies, and the recipes clipped or copied from the *Denver Post* or *Family Circle*.

The men talked about politics and war and occasionally lowered their voices to tell jokes that made them roar with laughter. Michael and Rodney played unenthusiastically at the back of the living room until Marge would tell Rodney to help Michael pick up the toys that he had dragged out or dumped onto the floor, and some wife would succeed in making eye contact with her husband long enough to persuade him to say, "Well, what do think, honey? Time to get going?"

Then there were early Sunday mornings, before Michael would wander in wanting to crawl into bed with us, or before Frisky the dog would bark to be let out, and before it was time to get ready to go to Mom and Dad's for Sunday dinner. It was in that crack in the dawn that, according to Gerry, we made love. It didn't seem like love to me. I don't even know what I thought at the time. Now I just remember it as bad sex. By bad, I don't mean evil, or even pleasantly naughty; I mean not good.

In the beginning, what I felt for Gerry was adulation, not love. I can't claim to know what he actually felt for me, but I believe it was somewhere between confusion and the ecstasy that might be derived from "a piece of liver in a knothole." As dehumanizing as that phrase seemed to me when Gerry first uttered it in an attempt to educate me about gender differences, I no longer take it personally, but it still seems demeaning of both men and women.

Until I started remembering Farragut and the partnership we had without dragging along everyone and everything else that ever had a claim on us, I didn't remember a period when we had actually enjoyed being together. I don't think we ever had another time when we developed the kind of commonality that allows strangers to blend as friends and lovers. But that is what I was looking for, hoping for, possibly even expected. I wanted a kind of melding, not just an itch and a scratch on Sunday morning. It was the very thing we didn't have.

1949 MEETING WHO I WANTED TO BE

Though we still lived on Pierson when I first took the job at Gates, we soon moved to central Denver, on Seventeenth Avenue, to an upstairs apartment in a duplex that had been split into four apartments. The neighborhood was rundown, probably because rent control was still on and owners couldn't afford to make repairs. Even now, somewhat gentrified, the old neglect shows through. It was a depressing place. The manager, who lived downstairs, always seemed to be spying through his partially open door, perhaps on guard against intruders. He didn't work, only managed the four apartments, that is, collected the rent. He claimed to be an artist. He drew very well, but he had only one subject, a single breast, very pretty, day after day, never a hand or a foot, just that one thing, that perfect breast. He valued his art but did not sell it so far as I know.

A sweet little boy named Dickie Tharp used to play outside, running back and forth on the sidewalk, yelling and laughing with the rest of the kids. His fingers were clubbed. A neighbor told me that Dickie had been born with a heart shaped like a boot. He was going to die and nothing at all could be done about it, so his parents decided to let him play all he could. And one day, he died; just stopped living his joyful little life.

Michael was three years old. He slept with his cowboy boots on. His hero was Hopalong Cassidy so Michael always dressed in black. One cold evening near the winter solstice when the big kids were still playing in the dark, Michael slipped downstairs and outside in his Hopalong Cassidy outfit. I was fixing dinner at the back of the apartment when the doorbell rang. It was the druggist from across the street. He was holding Hopalong by the hand. He said that Michael had crossed Seventeenth. "He could have been hit by the streetcar." I should have been watching him. "It gets dark early now. You gotta watch 'em all the time." Michael had seen some Hopalong Cassidy gloves in the store when I was in there buying cigarettes. His hands were cold.

Gerry worked nights at AAA. Sometimes he got off work early. He liked to creep up the stairs when I wasn't expecting him home, just to frighten me. He also liked to pin me down so I couldn't move until I panicked. Little things, always little things. I tried to leave him once, not long after my second baby. I went to my mother the first time he knocked me down. He hadn't hurt me, only demonstrated the fact that he could if he chose to. But my mother told me that one doesn't walk out on a marriage for a little thing like that. She said, "What would you do?" She asked me how I would support myself and Michael? I couldn't stay with her, even temporarily. There wasn't room. Besides, the thought of living with her had no appeal at all. Mother and I got on each other's nerves. We were always polite to each other without being especially kind. I needed a job.

Back in 1949, the Gates Rubber Company was the last place I ever thought I would apply for a job. It was that huge, ugly factory on the ugliest street in Denver, and it smelled bad. But I had few choices. I didn't want to be a housekeeper, a retail clerk in a department store, a file clerk, or a waitress; I took typing in junior high school but would have preferred not to. I did piece work for Wright McGill, tying flies, but never made my daily quota of sixteen dozen red ants. I had tried all of those occupations by the time I finished my after-school employment and summer breaks at East. My early work experience confirmed my growing suspicion that most women (as Thoreau put it) "lead lives of quiet desperation."

When I was in high school, the minimum wage was forty cents an hour. In 1949 President Truman raised it to seventy-five cents an hour, but that wouldn't go into effect until 1950. Meanwhile the lifting of wartime rent control wiped out the gain, as most landlords quickly doubled their rents. When I saw the Gates ad in the *Denver Post* in the Women's section of Help Wanted, I knew I had to try for it. They were looking for a woman under thirty; some college required; psychology major preferred; beginning salary of $147, plus benefits. Well, I didn't lie. I had some college, and when I took that psychology class, I was planning to either major or minor in psychology as part of my preparation for writing the great American novel that everyone had been waiting for. I had also read practically everything of importance that Freud ever wrote, that being *Interpretation of Dreams*.

I wore a hat and gloves, not for warmth; it was a warm day, but, in 1949, a hat and gloves were *de rigueur*. I filled out the application, being especially careful about my handwriting. Neatness counts, especially if one can't type more than twenty words a minute. Almost as soon as I submitted my application, Miss Maywood Graber, in personnel, called me in for an interview. The interview was brief but it was followed by an hour or so of testing in the personnel department. Miss Graber introduced me to a pleasant young woman named Page Stickney, who was to administer the necessary tests. Page gave me an eye exam on a machine called an Orthorator and one of us made a joke about the image of a red dotted line used to determine depth perception not being a red dotted lion. As she led me toward a row of small carrels, most of which were occupied, she

Gates Rubber Company, shortly before it was torn down, photo by Brad Bridgewater,
https://commons.wikimedia.org/wiki/File:Gates_Rubber,_gray.jpg

explained that the tests were only meant to match the applicant with the job, not to "grade or degrade." The first test, the "Wonderlic, "was the only one that was timed. She said that no one was expected to finish in the twelve minutes they were allotted. She seemed both cordial and efficient as she went through her duties. I could tell she was Southern, but her accent just smoothed the edges of her speech. I completed the testing with the "Washburne Social Adjustment Inventory" and the "Kuder Occupational Interest Survey." This was the basic battery of tests given to all applicants for clerical and professional positions.

Either my hat and white gloves or the results of my tests got me a job in the personnel department. I was to be a low-level psychometrist whose duties included administering and scoring the tests and entering accumulated data on a Friden calculator for the three psychometrists with degrees in psychology. Our supervisor may have had a degree, but his alleged expertise came from his WWII duty in the Office of Strategic Services (OSS), the forerunner of the CIA. If my application had been sent upstairs to a manager who had advertised in the morning paper he would have known that I was not really qualified to work in his air conditioned office.

The department skewed to white, and maybe a particular Wonderlic score. (The Wonderlic is a twelve-minute test based on the Stanford-Binet Test that is still used to determine the job placement of hundreds of thousands of applicants.) But had I been Black, no matter what real qualifications I had, a little numeral 1, 2, or 3 would have been placed in an innocuous square and I would never have been offered the Wonderlic pre-employment assessment, but a test the Army used in WWII for enlisted recruits, the Army General Classification Test (AGCT). The low numerals would have guaranteed a narrow scope of offerings within the company. I would "qualify" for a factory job, and not even a good one. I remember one tall, handsome, articulate man, with a fresh MA from DU. Even had he been coming from Harvard, being dark skinned he could have gotten a job in one of the departments where you had to stand in water all day, or the vulcanizing department where if you fell you could be chopped up and burned alive at the same time. Gates, like many "Northern" companies at the time, used skin color to decide who qualified for a mindless job in hellish heat. I felt angry about it. It was wrong and I knew it.

After working at Gates for a week or two, I was pretty sure I probably wouldn't like Page Stickney. I'm not the sort of person who goes out of my way to make friends, not just because I don't like being rejected but because I myself don't like many people, and if anybody is going to push someone away, it's going to be me doing the pushing. I hang back, observing and deciding what it is I just don't like about each person. I figured she was probably a Dixiecrat, the 1948 edition of a member of the "Tea Party" that emerged as a conservative backlash to voting in Barack Obama, the first Black president. Page always wore a little silver barrette in her hair with "Boo" engraved on it. When she left the South, she left her nickname behind—or meant to, but it didn't escape me. I assumed she approved of the unfairness of the little testing and judging regimen at Gates that we ourselves were both participating in and benefiting from.

Also, she talked a lot. Inane. I heard her going on and on about her shoes one day, explaining to Jane Begley, the other psychometrist, that she was wearing her "Bugsy" shoes. They had belonged to Virginia Hill, ice-hearted Bugsy Siegel's last girlfriend. She was his last because he had been riddled with bullets by intruders as he sat reading in her living room. Someone Page knew had known Virginia Hill before she became Bugsy's true love and he had named her Flamingo, way back in the days when she had no shoes and was just one the twelve kids of a dirt-poor Alabama family...blah blah blah...something like that. They were just ordinary, flat, beige-ish, tannish shoes—nothing that I would wear.

The day Page walked up to me, wearing her beige-ish, tannish Bugsy shoes and holding a blue personnel card in her hand, I thought I must have done something wrong. I had probably made some sort of mistake when I filled it out. Page had been charged with guarding the private information of people carefully chosen by our supervisor, in order to keep them from learning more than they should know about themselves—like their IQs. Fred Oberlander, had he not been a Jew, might have found a job a few years earlier devising statistical evidence that would justify the eradication of certain undesirables.

Page apparently had forgotten her charge and seemed excited to review some data that would eventually get turned into impersonal numbers and compared with the standards established by the members of the very department to which I had been assigned. She said she'd noticed that I was born September 7, 1927. I said, "Uh huh." She said she had been born on September 19, 1927. (I didn't say that I had a baby boy the day before her twenty-first birthday, but that he had died on the twenty-first day of September and last day of summer.) She said, with a question mark, I had been a member of PBF? I said that I had been a Pi Phi pledge but had not been initiated. (I didn't tell her that the day I went to campus looking for Gerry because I had heard he was back from wherever he had been hiding out after he returned from our supposed wedding trip, I had run into a friend from East High, who was a full-fledged Pi Phi who had asked me for my pledge pin back, allegedly because I wasn't enrolled in school for fall, but maybe because of my protruding belly.)

Page said she too had been a Pi Phi. At Sophie Newcomb, Tulane's women's college. I said that my husband had applied to Tulane's medical school. She said that her husband, Stone, had graduated from there and had just begun a psychiatric residency at Colorado Psychopathic Hospital, then a part of the University of Colorado Medical School. She said that all of our test scores were very close: interests, personality traits, everything with one exception. She said our Wonderlic scores were within a few percentiles but were not exactly the same. I probably said, "Yeah?" or maybe, "Huh!"

Fred, who had been a Master Sergeant in the OSS, and was now the master of our fate, knew the importance of *esprit de corps*. He liked to invite his employees and their spouses to small, informal dinners in his home, to meet "the wife," and get to know each other outside of the office. Having noted the similarities on those blue personnel cards, he invited the Stickneys and McClards on the same evening. It was an awkward evening, at least in my mind. I don't remember much beyond my own self-consciousness. The Stickneys were at ease, comfortable with themselves, entertaining, Stone, handsome in a Brooks Brothers seersucker suit, Page—I don't remember what she wore, only that when she took her glasses off, to wipe them, her large, blue-green eyes stunned me. I had never even noticed how beautiful she was. I'd noticed she was left-handed and wrote in an awkward, left-handed way, and I'd noticed that she had a certain way of walking in her Bugsy shoes, and that she wore that Boo pin in her light brown hair, and had a little tilt to her head when she wrote.

Michael dressed as Hopalong Cassidy on porch of our house on 17ᵗʰ Avenue

She probably noticed that I was a chain-smoker of Lucky Strikes, and that Gerry's fingernails still had a little dirt under them from working on the car, even though he'd scrubbed them almost raw.

They were storytellers, collectors of oddments. We were bumpkins and I was certain that the Stickneys now held about the same disregard for Westerners as I had for Southerners, the difference being that they regarded us as the primitives they had actually hoped to observe. I assumed they had hoped to see, if not cowboys and Indians, at least a few prospectors and big-hearted whores, but we were close enough. Using Page's vocabulary, I am referring to "regional differences." Using my own, the term would be "local color." I felt decidedly under par.

Ironically, my mother, the same woman whose tragic flaw was a vanity that aspired to the appearance of superiority or even aristocracy, had taught me that sophistication was not the same as wisdom. She said it was more closely related to sophistic than sophic. It was about appearance rather than substance. The occasion of making the distinction was to tell me that a person who hadn't even received her high school diploma that night, when she paraded across the stage in her cap and gown was just a know-nothing with smokers' breath and a Ronson lighter. It was good instruction, though how Mother used this knowledge to defend her own ego I am not sure. Page and Stone seemed to have wisdom, to be the real thing, and I had no diploma. Sitting in the Oberlanders' living room that evening there was, no doubt, something falsely reassuring about hiding in a cloud of curling smoke. I was like a two-year-old, hiding behind a curtain that was too short to cover my bare feet.

However it was that I came into Page's field of vision, had we been born identical twins, it would have been difficult to learn anything of importance about each other had we not been required to eat together several times a week by the rigidly enforced lunch schedule. Even then, we might never have had an inkling that we found each other both serious and amusing had we not both been unusually fast eaters.

It wasn't that Page didn't have a great deal to learn that I already knew. Page had never been a bored housewife. She had gone directly from being a debutante, to being a Pi Phi, to being a college graduate, to being a doctor's wife. She had never thought she felt a little twitch, that might just have been gas, that turned out to be a kind of parasite that made her throw up if she smelled food and grew into something that kicked and turned and hiccupped and turned out not to be part of her at all, but someone else, for whom she would be forever responsible and love more than she loved her own life. She had never been disgraced, dismissed, or humiliated for being young and full of life. She was as ignorant as I was, just more respectable.

Stone was Gerry's age but had graduated from medical school two years before Gerry started in premed. While Gerry was dive-bombing during the war, noticing how the red roof tiles seemed to explode as his rounds hit them and sometimes seeing what might have been Brownian motion of particles under a microscope, Stone was in the Navy's V-12 program at Tulane's medical school, and sitting around listening to jazz and learning to drink like a southerner—"slow and steady"—in the French Quarter with his roommate, Ted Cary, Page's brother. Page had earned her BA in psychology the year Stone finished his internship. In 1948, while I was borrowing maternity dresses, or wearing Gerry's old shirt over my unzipped jeans, Page had been planning a simple traditional wedding. Then, instead of taking a cramped, isolated apartment after a honeymoon, they had decided to store their wedding gifts of sterling and china and sail off on a tramp steamer to Paris where Stone served a second internship at American University Hospital. So, I was surprised the next week when Page invited us to dinner and even asked us to bring Michael, our almost-three-year-old son.

They lived at 22 Lincoln in a tiny, wonderfully messy, attic apartment. Stone played the guitar and sang American and British folk songs in his soft, sweet Alabama accent. He sang to Michael. "The Fox," "Mr. Rabbit," the Burl Ives repertoire. The only other song I remember from that night is "Eggs, eggs, and marrow bones will make your old man blind/But if you want for to do him in, sneak up from behind." Meanwhile, Page was making dinner on a two-burner gas stove. She made a crab gumbo from the only crab in Denver, one big Dungeness. Years later, Stone was still chiding her about the one-crab gumbo. After dinner, she made Try Me chicory coffee in a white enamel drip pot and served it in demitasses. The silver spoon shone deep red at the bottom. I don't think I ever made another tea-colored cup of coffee.

I loved everything about the evening, but most of all I remember being happy that they seemed to enjoy Michael. Afterward, Page said she had been around several children the same age and none had been as advanced, so verbal. Gerry commented on how comfortable they both were to be around. He liked both of them. I saw them as having the kind of marriage I wanted, living the kind of life I wanted. It was the kind of evening I wanted to spend, the kind of conversation I wanted to participate in. It was never stuffy, never pedantic, never boastful, never condescending, always inclusive. They were both gracious, seeming to value what others said.

Page, it turned out, was neither Southern stereotype I held in my mind, neither Scarlet O'Hara nor Blanche DuBois. She had absorbed and been absorbed by Europe, the museums, the opera, the theater, the ballet.

During her school years, she had also read most, if not all, of the Twentieth Century American and French novelists. Oh, and she had read all of Collette, which gave her a certain piquancy. She had also read Havelock Ellis, which could have been her source of information about exactly what it was that lesbians do. As an adult, she was an inveterate reader of newspapers, the *Times Picayune, Manchester Guardian*, Sunday *New York Times*, and the local paper (which was at that moment the *Denver Post*.) The only magazines she read regularly were the *New Yorker*, and the *New Republic*.

I've never known anyone at all like Page. She frequently said that she wasn't the least bit creative. She wasn't a maker. She imagined she wasn't gifted because she didn't make art of any sort. Her gift was in her understanding of all forms of art—and people. There was nothing superficial about her, no affectation, no feigning. She was the perfect audience (without which no art would really exist). And she was generous. She made me feel that I had value. She would take something normal I had said and in allegedly quoting it to someone else so enhance it that it seemed brilliant.

Usually, when I examine the memories I've stored away so carefully, I see that events and people were not what they had seemed to be at the time. When I dust them off I find, as with Juneau, or even Mrs. Wood, what treasures they left me with. You can't know anyone for twenty years and think about them for another forty and imagine them to be perfect, but it comes to be that the flaws become just characteristics, features, no longer their primary identifiers. I would come to know full well that the Stickney marriage was not at all as it appeared to be, at least as miserable as Gerry's and mine, and Page and Stone were both as flawed as we were, but what I learned in even imagining knowing them helped me to respect myself, to love and be loved.

Both Page and Stone still stand there, looking as they always did. I might even still fall goofily in love with the one I had so wanted to emulate. The difference would be that I would not detest myself for imagining that another person could somehow complete me. I would never say to her, as a warning, "I always seem to love the wrong people." I was a good deal older when I realized that I had almost let the impropriety of my feelings keep me from falling in love, but "falling in love" is not a voluntary act. I guess there might be a little aura, like the scotoma that precedes a migraine or a grand mal. In some cases, one might be able to avoid the thing; however, I will be forever grateful that I just went ahead with it all.

1950 - 59 Getting to Know Page

By the time we became friends with the Stickneys, Gerry had graduated from DU and been accepted at University of Colorado School of Medicine. Less than a month after his graduation, on June 25, 1950, North Korea crossed the thirty-eighth parallel. The Doctor Draft begun in WWII was reinstated. Stone had resigned his Navy Reserve commission when he graduated from Tulane and went to Paris, but as an MD he was eligible to be drafted into the Army during the Korean War. If I remember correctly, within six weeks, he was sent to Japan where he was assigned to the psychiatric ward of a large military hospital in Yokohama. Had he been a surgeon he would have been assigned to a MASH unit in Korea.

I was surprised when Page decided to stay in Denver while she waited to hear whether the Army would provide her transportation to Japan. I urged her to return to New Orleans but she insisted that she really didn't want to. Although she loved and respected her widowed mother, she felt that her mother was domineering. She said that her mother had chosen every other friend she had ever had and was still trying to control her and her brother Ted. So, for whatever actual reason, Page stayed on in Denver (albeit with friends of her mother) until a short time after the Army

Page and Stone in Italy

cleared her for travel to Japan. I felt as though my life was ending as I watched her pack to return to New Orleans. I didn't think I would ever hear from her again. I thought she would forget me as soon as she stepped off the plane in New Orleans.

A few days after she left, I went into our one clothes closet, reached under a folded blanket on the top shelf and felt for the thirty-two caliber Colt revolver Gerry kept there. I had never held a gun before. I cocked it and I stood with it pressed against my temple, not wanting to die, just not wanting to live. But I thought of my beautiful little boy and what it would mean to abandon him in what I believed was a loveless world. I disarmed the gun and replaced it back under the blanket. Remembering that very private moment in a closet in an empty apartment, I sometimes wonder about my own authenticity, that is, had it not been for Michael, would I actually have pulled the trigger? Might I have ended my own life and deprived my yet-to-exist descendants of theirs for no better reason than being alone?

During the two years the Stickneys lived in Japan, Page and I wrote long letters to each other. I probably wrote about Michael. She wrote detailing life in Tokyo, where they lived in a paper house and cooked on a hibachi—charming letters on occasion, not to Gerry or me, but to Michael. Page taught English to the young girls at Tokyo Peer School, the school attended by the children of the Japanese aristocracy. She must have been successful in her attempts to teach them. After returning to the United States, she received several letters from her former students. I remember a pretty little note from a girl who said that she and her classmates all missed her and her "amusing antics." (I have always hoped that someday I would meet a native Japanese woman who spoke English with a refined New Orleans Accent.)

Page and I wrote to each other every day for many years, only tapering to less often than that in the year or so before she died. Once she was back from Japan, in the United States, we talked on the phone fairly frequently. It was my only real indulgence because long distance telephone was very expensive then. We loved to hear each other's stories, to make each other laugh.

Page was spontaneous and funny. She said of herself that she was not a wit, but a clown. She was very verbal, quick-witted, more pithy than witty. That is, she never strived to be clever for the sake of display. She had a ready store of *mots justes*. And she was a clown, a mime. I remember ten-month-old Peter, sitting happily amidst pans he'd pulled from her kitchen cupboard, swinging a small skillet, scythe-like, right at her shins. She leaped. He swung. She leaped. He swung. She leaped and turned. It was a pan dance.

Page had many lovely friends. She was always running into someone she hadn't seen since Paris or Boston or Kyoto. The first time I went to New York with her, we twice ran into men who were walking toward us and suddenly called, "Boo?" her New Orleans nickname, or "Page Stickney! I can't believe it." They embraced and chattered, writing down addresses, and sent regards to spouses. I teased her about her ubiquitous friends. Later, as we sat at a table outside The Cloisters museum up in Washington Heights, I had to wonder, with so many lovely friends, why she had chosen me to be her confidante, her frequent companion, not yet her lover.... Oh, but I *would* have been, had I dared risk losing her as a friend, or, more likely having her laugh at the joke. Then I would have to laugh too. She said it was true that she had many friends but "Not many people are *fun*." As it turns out, much of loving another mortal isn't fun either. It was Page from whom I first heard, "Life gives us moments, and for those moments we give our lives."

* * *

Page was both a private person and devoted to "keeping up appearances." I had known very early that her father had died when she was eight years old, but it was many years later that I learned that eight-year-old Page had come home from school to a confusing scene of grieving friends. She had been told only that her father was "gone." Perhaps a well-meaning person had said that he had "passed away," or gone to heaven. She told me that she felt he had abandoned her. Much later she learned that he had committed suicide, shot himself, apparently in his despair over bankruptcy during the height of the depression. Her mother, Enid Ewing Cary, had then taken Page to Southern California, leaving ten-year-old Ted in the care of "Boots, Enid's cousin." I don't know for how long, or why to California. When they returned, it was not to Beaumont but to New Orleans.

I'd known the Stickneys for about nine years before I got a more realistic view of their marriage. They had already lived in Pittsburgh for several years when we moved east, first to Pennsauken, Pennsylvania, a couple of weeks after Elizabeth was born, and three years after that to Portsmouth, Virginia, where Peter would be born. Over those five and a half years our two families joined each other for many special occasions, and Page and I once took a trip to New York City by ourselves. But it was specifically from our private conversation at Rehoboth Beach that I learned the most about the failure of their marriage.

Both of the Stickneys helped me become a better parent and all-around better person than I would have been otherwise. Stone was always wonderful with Michael, by far the best man in Michael's life. Michael revered his dad. Gerry loomed large, was handsome, and important, but it was Stone who sang to him, showed him how to shuck oysters and eat them, how to catch blue crabs with turkey necks. He took Michael hunting and fishing, and let him drive his jeep, but most importantly Stone was supportive, treated him like he was a real person. Gerry believed people weren't worth talking to until they were whatever age he was.

* * *

When I finally left Gerry, Page was one of two people who encouraged me when I got the crazy idea of going back to school in 1963, when a thirty-five-year-old freshman was still an oddity. Mother predicted that I wouldn't finish, because I was "just like Chaunce," never finishing anything. Mardie crossed me off her Christmas card list. Mr. McClard told me there was no need for me to go back to school. It had been all right, he said, for me to work when Gerry was in school, but I had plenty of money to live on without going back to school and if I *didn't* have, I could probably work as a menial—a waitress or housekeeper.

Me in the spring of 1960, holding my youngest son, Peter

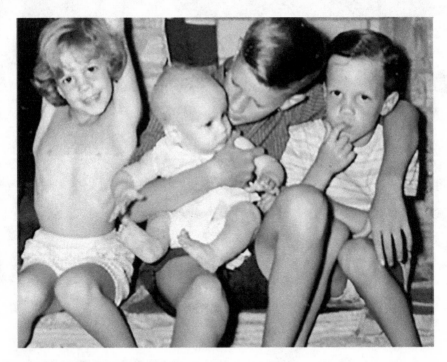

My four oldest children, Liz, Peter, Michael, and Kevin, 1960

Anne, my youngest, and my mother, around the time that our divorce was finalized, 1963

1962 THE END OF OUR MARRIAGE

Gerry had never learned how to drink. He wasn't an alcoholic; he just
wasn't a good drinker. He drank like a college kid who had never had a
drink in his life and then saw it as a competition to show that he could
handle any amount of liquor. But downing a few drinks didn't make him
happy; it just released his rage, his frustration. The same stuff that, when
trained and perfectly controlled, allowed Dr. McClard, the surgeon, to cut
precisely into the belly of a patient and remove or repair the offending
organ. Perhaps when it was untethered it had allowed him to swoop down
on small villages and fire hundreds of rounds at the scurrying little people
beneath him, no bigger than ants.

   I really think the biggest part of our problem was that Gerry finally
opted to see me as his parents and their generation saw me, as inferior to
him for just being a woman, yet he was bothered by somehow knowing
that that was not true. Maybe it gave him nightmares for the same
reasons he had nightmares about those scurrying little people that he had
killed that looked like ants but weren't. He told me that I was "too smart
to be a woman," and on numerous occasions I embarrassed him by
proffering my opinion on a man's topic, uninvited. I believed not only

that a man should be kind and thoughtful, well informed, emancipated from his parents, and responsible, but that he should be able to infer what I wanted or needed from the most oblique reference. Maybe both of us had such bizarre expectations of what a "real" woman or a "real" man was or might be capable of being that we not only hated each other but ourselves too...for having chosen such defective mates. And there we were, just two human beings who got all tangled up in our own nonsense.

That night, so long ago, he was very drunk and very angry and I thought he was going to kill me. Worse, I believed the children were in grave danger. He was completely out of control. As his hands tightened around my neck, instinct told me that if he became further agitated, if he succeeded in killing me, he would go after the children. I knew how easily a family could become a headline about a domestic massacre, then nothing at all. I didn't struggle. He released me, then threw me on the bed, bit me again and again, raped me, let me go, then followed me into the hall, grabbed me, pinned me against the wall with his thumb in my eye and held me there. I heard Elizabeth stir. I told her to go back to sleep, that it was just a dream. Gerry released me, and moved off, making strange, half-crying sounds like a wounded beast. I could hear him ransacking the closets, I suspected, in search of a revolver that had been stolen five years before, mercifully, on our move to New Jersey.

Fifteen-year-old Michael, who was in his bedroom, heard the awful, hurt animal sounds. Long after that night, he told me he couldn't tell whether his father was laughing or crying. He hadn't known what to do. He wondered if he could get to the twenty-two rifle on his closet shelf. How would he load it? Because he hadn't heard me, he feared that I was dead, so he waited, powerless, wondering if he could shoot his father—if he should, if he would.

I stood in the kitchen for what seemed a long time. I had put on a raincoat to cover my nakedness, not knowing how to get help, how to open the door without being heard, and not willing to leave the children alone. He came into the kitchen, quiet now, as though he had awakened from a nightmare. He told me, with seeming admiration, that I was "calm under fire." I told him that was only so because I knew he was a good a man, and that his native decency would stop him.

I'm pretty sure that if he had killed me, a 1962 jury would have sympathized with him, perhaps even let him off entirely. He was a doctor. He was a naval officer, and a gentleman. He had good reason. I was a lesbian, wasn't I? I had admitted that I was in love with a woman. Loving someone that society says is the wrong person is evil. Vile. Unspeakable.

And the thing that troubled me so, the thing that I felt so ashamed of for so long: loving and being loved by, being happy with, grieving with, nurturing, and being nurtured by another human being? I came to recognize it as an incredible gift. As Page once said in response to Gerry's having called our friendship pathological, "Then, here's to pathology!" Pathological or not, it was Page and Stone who helped me get out of a truly sick relationship. My mother perceived us as "such a beautiful couple," and my sister, Mardie, who had once said, "If a man ever hit me, that would be it," still, considered me as a fool for leaving a marriage I had such a large investment in.

Yes, our marriage was an enormous mistake, but I have no regrets other than those one always has at failure. I am very thankful for it. I can't imagine my life without my children, each and all, exactly as they are.

Gerry and his second wife should have been thankful, too. He got through eight years of school, an internship, a four-year residency, plus his brief post-residency time in Portsmouth before being freed to travel the world without the encumbrance of children. When the children had all grown into lovely, educated people, they loved, respected, and forgave him for any shortcomings he might have had. His second marriage lasted for thirty years. He had a great life and probably even realized it before he died.

Looking back, it's so much easier to understand life as the privilege it is—just living on our beautiful earth, for however long, because "for however long," is always Now.

1969 Page, Death

I was running late that day; I was stuffing the reader for freshman composition and the stack of papers I had just finished grading into my bag. My kids were walking to school, perhaps on the bridge over the Valley Highway. Old worries linger. Perhaps I had been patting my pocket for the keys, wondering why I had the feeling I had forgotten something.

When the phone rang, I knew, no, hoped it would be Page. I always loved to hear her voice, even for a moment, but I hesitated, almost not answering. I couldn't be late for my class. Students wait fifteen minutes for full professors but not fifteen seconds for teaching fellows.

When I finally picked up the phone, her sigh-tinged "Good morning" betrayed her mood. I didn't ask what was wrong. I didn't really want to get into whatever it was. I was already late. She asked if I had received the Updike poem. I probably paused before answering. I remembered there was something else in the letter she had sent a day or so before. To avoid lying, I probably said, "Yes. I love Updike. Thank you." Something like that. She would have recognized the evasion. I might have read it quickly and not thought about it beyond the moment. (The truth is that yesterday, as I was looking through my big file of old letters for my father's one letter to me, I found two items, pressed together, that I don't remember ever

Page with her son, Cary, at the pool, circa 1960

having seen before, the folded poem and a soiled, post-office change-of-address card for Page Stickney. I know that poem has long been buried in my heart.)

I had been disappointed when Page decided to follow Stone to his new job in Montgomery, Alabama. It seemed even further away from me than Pittsburgh. She was moving away from a familiar place, one I could visualize, one I had shared for a short time, people that I knew—and that she loved. She was torn, and she was angry. And this was the time, if there was ever a time, that she might have made the split. It would have been so easy, simply to stay there in her home. So much of her life's matter was there in Squirrel Hill, and before that in Wilkinsburg. Her children, Cary and Morgan, now eleven and thirteen, had both been born there. My daughter, Anne, had been born there eight years before. Stone had built a practice there.

Moving to Montgomery meant moving away from a wealth of friends, dear friends with whom she had shared so much of life, small triumphs, the first words, the first steps, the first days of school, the children's birthday parties; the small miseries, runny noses, temper tantrums, bee-stings, hangovers. These were friends who shared her convictions and concerns, friends who had marched with her. Her friends had rallied around her during her two-year convalescence from the terrible automobile accident. They had mourned the deaths of Emmett Till, John F. Kennedy, Martin Luther King Jr., Bobby Kennedy. They admired Rosa Parks and hated George Wallace.

She'd been in Pittsburgh since 1953, the year the Stickneys came through Denver on their way home from Japan. When they told us where they were headed, I questioned why anyone would move to such a terrible place. Having never been east of Colorado, all I knew about Pittsburgh was that huge steel mills with smokestacks produced foul air. Also, a terrible thing had happened in a nearby town. About a month after John Christopher was born, there was a big story in the *Denver Post* about thousands of people being sickened by factory smoke in Donora. Two dozen of them had died. The government had been looking into the cause for about five years. Congress was talking about new regulations. In my mind, a layer of thick smoke blanketed the entire Commonwealth of Pennsylvania.

So I was surprised in 1955, when we visited the Stickneys on our way to Gerry's surgical residency in Philadelphia. A blue sky was evident beyond the steep hills and tree-lined streets. The warm summer days yielded to cool summer nights. The industry that had previously cast such a shadow over the area had cleaned itself up significantly, years before the federal government finished its investigation of the 1948 Donora tragedy— and almost two decades before the Environmental Protection Agency was established. Pittsburgh's steel manufacturers had not been motivated by altruism. It was just good business. Scientists and engineers from all over the world flocked to the area.

In addition to the physical atmosphere, Page had found the best political climate she had ever experienced. Her new community shared her values, but the old wealth informed them. The arts were Page's lifeline.

When I first met Page, she frequently spoke of "regional differences." Often she was referring to superficial practices such as degree of formality. She said that northern women were "brash." I don't think she meant we were impetuous. I think she meant we were too forward or possibly less tactful than Southern women. Or maybe she meant that we were arrogant. She, like most Southerners, greatly resented our assumption that racism was a Southern phenomenon. It never was, of course, but it is so much easier to recognize faults in others than in ourselves. To me, "segregation" meant *laws* that denied Negro children the right to attend the same schools that whites attended. We had no such laws where I had lived, but the neighborhoods I had lived in were completely segregated. Even the working-class neighborhood in southwest Los Angeles where the Woods lived was pure white. Northern injustices were just as much there, but disguised, kept invisible to those who weren't the objective losers. The only Negroes I ever saw on West Seventieth Street were the men who stood on the back of the garbage truck. Raymond Avenue Grammar School was white (with the exception of Sachiko). The only Negro I had ever actually spoken to before I was grown was the porter who helped me into the upper berth of the Pullman car on my way to Billings.

When I was in junior high, I once ran in terror from a group of Negro girls in Exposition Park. They had yelled some insult at me, and fearing they would beat me to death, I had run until I was completely out of breath. When I gave up, they were nowhere in sight. They were probably still standing in the same place, doubled over in laughter.

During the fifteen years the Stickneys lived in Western Pennsylvania, America had undergone enormous internal changes, many of which were the unfinished business of the Civil War. I had been aware of the injustices I saw around me, but mine was a passive awareness. I knew Jim Crow laws were cruel and humiliating, but gee, what was wrong with sitting in the back of the bus? I mean, I sat back there lots of times. I thought it was a shame that the Manual High School football team, only a mile or so from East Denver High School, was so poor that they wore their old uniforms until they fell apart. But that was just because they were poor, not because they were Negroes. And I felt really bad about that fellow with his new MA from DU, who did so well on the AGCT, but I had to work in a factory once, tying trout flies. A summer job is a summer job. As mortified as I am now to admit it, I didn't see any real malice in words like "jigaboo" or "spook" either. Jerome Biffle, one of the twelve Negro kids at East when I was there, and the star running back on East's fantastic football team was a "spook," but we all loved him. I knew that my own mother wouldn't eat lunch with her best friend at work, who was a "lovely person even though she was a Negress." Although I never heard Mother refer directly to a Negro that way, she once referred to me as a "nigger lover," for supporting the Civil Rights Movement. Many kids routinely referred to the topmost balcony in movie theaters as "nigger heaven." That was just an expression.

Long before I lived in Portsmouth, Virginia, I came to recognize all of that as racist and demeaning, but somehow still less important than what went on in the South. I hated to hear about the separate restrooms, separate water fountains, separate entrances to theaters. I knew that Jean, the young mother of two children, who cleaned my house lived in Cavalier Manor, a project built next to the Portsmouth city dump. (I have to believe the pun was deliberate rather than coincidental.)

I was shocked when Jean said, "I can shop all day at any department store, but I can't even get a glass of water at the lunch counter." I didn't like it, but I accepted it as the status quo. I believed, as so many ignorant people do, that given time, it would change. When the sit-ins at lunch counters began in Norfolk, stories appeared in the newspaper about police in other places having used attack dogs to discourage the practice. I was more afraid of the escalation of violence in my neighborhood than of the daily violence of racism endured by its victims. It's not hard to be passive when you are not the victim.

Page, who had been born in Beaumont, Texas, moved to New Orleans while still in grade school and lived there about as long as she lived in Pittsburgh. She had been cared for by Black hands all of her life. They had tended her needs as a child, cooked her food, washed her clothes, and kept her home tidy. She had known the paternalism of the South, the American form of noblesse oblige. She well understood that powerless people have few, if any, of the resources they need to save themselves. I don't know when she learned that it always takes energy to overcome inertia. Page embraced the Civil Rights Movement. I welcomed the idea of Civil Rights, too, but I feared the Movement.

Page was never a good driver. She was nearsighted and loved to speed—not an especially good combination. One night as she was heading home after stopping at Georgia's for dinner, she plowed into a left-turning car. No one in the other car was hurt, but Page's face was crushed when it hit the steering wheel. Georgia saw her soon after she was brought into the emergency room, conscious but unrecognizable. When I asked Georgia about Page's condition, she simply said, "I threw up." And Page herself reported hearing a passenger on the hospital elevator saying, "We shouldn't have to look at that." I didn't see her until several weeks later, when I was needed to fill in during her convalescence. I was shocked, even then, to see an unfamiliar face, with nothing quite the same, and find her spirit wounded, needy.

But she had never been alone during her long recovery that included two years of plastic surgery. She had the support of many good friends. Ted Fenton was one of the most important. He was a bright, caring young history professor at Carnegie-Mellon, who had initiated a Master of Arts in Teaching program in which he hoped to "get those bright, highly educated women off the streets and into classrooms." He was referring to women who literally spent their days carpooling station wagons full of kids to school and after-school activities, while the schools hired people with certification in teaching methods and weak minors in the subjects they taught. Ted recruited both Page's good friend and neighbor in Squirrel Hill, Georgia, and Page for the new program. For Page, the opportunity came as she was reconstructing herself after the accident. She had just settled into her teaching career when Stone's career blew up in his face. Six years had passed since her terrible accident. She had grown accustomed to her remodeled face. She loved her job, teaching children with assorted learning disorders. She loved the children, six and seven years old, each with challenging issues. She had learned American Sign Language. She hadn't wanted to leave them.

But...in spite of everything, all the hurt, she loved Stone. She was angry with him, furious, even, before he destroyed his career as a psychoanalyst, but for her his best qualities equaled if not outweighed his worst. As she had said, "I love going on his arm to the symphony." Appearances.

She said, "Stone's done it again. I can't take it any longer." She wasn't crying. She wasn't a crier. No matter how upset she might be, she would never make a scene in public. She once said that the angrier she was the nicer she became. But off stage she freed her demons. I once saw her fling a Haviland cup like a fastball to shatter against the kitchen wall. She had planned a Twelfth Night party for weeks and selected the guests with care, old friends and interesting newcomers she hoped to get to know better. The party was a great success. Most of the guests were sitting in small groups, laughing, talking, a few standing at the self-service bar, and two or three couples dancing; among them, the host dancing with the attractive wife of one of the newcomers to their social scene. Page was happily wandering through the crowd, serving hors d'oeuvres and chatting until she spotted Stone's errant right hand loosening the chignon at the nape of his partner's neck, allowing her dark hair to fall free to sway with the music.

Neither of the dancers heard the small crash in the kitchen.

Page tolerated rather than forgave Stone for his many lapses. But she, like even the most tolerant, kept a tally. So many times, so much suppressed rage, so much need to "maintain appearances." Finally, the threat of a malpractice suit for the alleged seduction of one of his patients, with a second suit on the horizon, was beyond her capacity. It had nullified more than seven years of analytic training.

Stone liked to refer to psychoanalytic training as "the new monasticism," but monasticism implies a kind of seclusion, a peaceful time for contemplation and scholarship—in a monastery. Stone lived at the center of a household in the middle of a scurrying city and the contemplation of self was not limited to his navel. His long training analysis consisted primarily of five years of intensive psychoanalysis during which he was necessarily self-absorbed and "acting out." All of his demons were freed to run rampant through the entire community, in a kind of prolonged exorcism meant to result in the clarity of vision that would allow him to free his patients of their own demons. But, once freed, the demons apparently took over his household and rode on his shoulders to work.

To Page, the real and terrible loss of Stone's right to practice psychiatry meant disaster. She lost her home, her community, her standing. The move to Montgomery, Alabama, where Stone was hired to bring the state's mental health facilities into compliance with federal law, was devastating. It meant the loss of meaningful political activism. Page was a passionate liberal Democrat. In 1963, she had been part of the "March on Washington." She had been there to hear Martin Luther King call out, "I have a dream...."

As time went on, I sometimes felt that I had become the safety valve that allowed her to maintain a kind of equilibrium in an unhealthy relationship. I was also a complication—and I was gradually being relieved as a source of either healing or palliation as her drinking increased.

Once the matter of my supposed education came up in an odd way. She said she felt that I had surpassed her. That was in no way true. How could she have imagined that even for a moment? I had only been trying to become a person with something to give back and to give forward to my children and the students I would soon have to face, pretending to know something of importance, something they might have some use for.

We had planned for her to visit Denver in March but something had come up. She wanted me to visit Montgomery instead. I said I couldn't possibly, because I didn't have the money and even if I did, arranging for childcare on such short notice would be difficult.

She had told me in a previous call that their house, named Wisdomwood by its previous owner, a "Fitzgerald kind of house," had a pecan grove in front of it. Of course, we laughed about the psychiatrist growing nuts in a place called Wisdomwood. But she said that it was drafty and she could never get warm. Her hands were always cold. She mentioned her disappointment with a sorority sister who had made no effort to introduce her to women in the community.

I told her that I really had to get to class.

I was impatient with her as she went on about Stone's latest adventure. I said, "But you know you had a choice and you chose to move to Montgomery." I like to think I said it with kindness, but I don't believe there is a way to say such a thing with kindness.

I said, "I'm so sorry, Page, but I really have to go."

"But when will I see you?"

I answered, "I guess, when we meet on that beautiful shore," a line from the gospel hymn "In The Sweet Bye And Bye." I was alluding to Sandbridge, where they had just finished building their beach house. Shortly before I left Gerry, just before the Ash Wednesday storm, we, Gerry and I, and the Stickneys had both bought beachfront lots there, just south of Virginia Beach.

"I really must go. I'll call this afternoon when I get back from campus."

All day, I regretted my impatience. There had rarely, if ever, been a time that Page had failed to support me. I knew full well how unhappy she was, how lonely. As soon as I got home, I called to apologize. A woman's voice said, "Mrs. Stickney isn't home." I asked her if she would tell her that Megan called.

"I'm Valerie, her next-door neighbor.... There's been an accident. She's...." I don't know what I said or what I might have asked in the long pause, I was expecting to hear that she had been taken to the emergency room. But the sentence didn't end that way. Just the one word, isolated, hanging in the void.

"Dead."

I suppose everyone on earth has known or will know that moment beyond despair, when the world seems to fall away, and there is no undoing, no possibility, no forgiveness...and the moment that follows, when one realizes the world of commitment and necessity is still there in its entirety to be dealt with. The children. The dinner, the garbage, the dog, preparation for another day and yet another. The somehow being.

Liz home. Screaming.

Stone called. A tree. She had been alone. Hit a tree.... Maybe she was trying to avoid something on the road.... Skid marks.... Swerved.... Car flew through...air.... Hit a tree.... Car broke in two.... Page, her...head.... Wrong car."

I remember sitting numb through poetry workshop the next day, until Pawlowski called on me to read the draft of a poem I'd handed in the week before. I only remember one line now, but the poem was about a meteorite, a shooting star, "falling to earth to lie with common field stone." I started to read it, but lost control, bursting into tears.

Mary Shumway must have followed me out of the room as I left class. I don't remember. I know I told her. She took me home to her apartment, where I cried myself empty away from the children.

And then I remember being on the plane and looking down at the billowing, bright tops of the clouds and thinking aloud that they looked firm enough to walk on. The man next to me said, "I don't think you should try it."

I think Michael and Judy watched the children. I don't know who.

And then an eternity or an instant later I was in the Atlanta airport and Stone was there with—for a moment—Page. *It was all a mistake or a dream.* She turned into fourteen-year-old Cary.

Then there was a house full of people, milling around with drinks, mainly people I knew from Pittsburgh, but one or two whose names and stories I had only heard, from New Orleans, the ones who only knew her as Boo. Page's closest friend from schooldays in New Orleans glared at me but we never spoke. Stone's mother, who had worn black to her son's wedding, signifying his death by marriage, was there. She carried a tiny toy poodle during most of two days. In my mind at least, she was holding it when she peered into the hole in which the urn was or was not. Ted Fenton, without his wife, Barbara, whose loosened hair as she had danced with Stone once occasioned the throwing of a cup, was among the comforters. Neighbors brought cakes with coconut frosting. So many sweet white cakes. Flowers, gladiolus, everywhere. At some point, Cary had said to me, he wished the guests would remember how funny Page was. No one was laughing, just talking and drinking.

The brief service was held in Grace Episcopal Church, a tiny church just large enough to contain the group of mourners. I don't remember the music Stone chose; I only remember her once expressing regret that moving to Alabama would mean she would probably never again hear "The Battle Hymn of the Republic." I thought as I sat there, how grand it would have been to hear "where the grapes of wrath are stored."

Some thirty years later, on the day of Stone's funeral, a March wind wrenched a tree from its footing in the churchyard and smashed it into Grace Church.

The mills of the gods do grind slow...and fine.

Stone asked me if I would come down on spring break and go through Page's things, decide what to send where. And make arrangements for Morgan, Page's and Stone's other young son, eleven at the time.

P.S. You may be amused by some of the latest controversies — enclosed.

4/29/69

Megan,

Thanks for your letter of 21 April & your good words. Of course I'll be a godfather to Peter, & help drive the devil out as the Episcopalians say. I have lost my skepticism, cynicism, &c. about the ultimate mysteries — except I now apply them toward the revealed wisdom of the scientific establishment, which has no answers to the truly hard questions. Anyway, I am honored, and will probably be a better spiritual guide than some. (who?) Don't rush on the decoration of Page's gravestone. There is plenty of time. I am very glad

you are helping me with it. And I'm
sorry you've hurt your hand. Or
anything else. Get well soon.
"Megan I love your constancy   (Dan! Eddie
To her, to hers, to me.   creeps in)
In your brown gaze, occasionally
We are what we could be." No apolo-
gies for this effusion. Spontaneous.
Also, gratitude for how you helped
me, or let us help each other. Who
else could?
Keep me posted on details for Sandbridge — the boys & I look forward
to that time with you & Tia & Page
& Gigi & Kevin & Mike. Remember, The
place sleeps 12 without using cots,
sofas, sleeping bags, et.
As to Strategy — forget it, & your
triumphs over faculty. No bar taken
Charlotte. Need I say more?
                        love, Jane

2007 Mexico

Paraìso Perdido

At some time during the week, everyone at the family reunion had uttered the word "paradise." "Everyone" is an exaggeration. Soren and Solian, the eight- and six-year-old *angeles* hadn't even noticed they were in Akumal. They had taken a quick peek at Tulum, but not long enough to ask a single question about the ruins. Once they were settled in our rented villa, *La Yardena*, they only looked up from their little game boxes long enough to test the desserts. For the rest of us, just looking out at the perfect aquamarine sea that lapped at sand beyond the palm trees, or walking through the tropical garden that buffered our world from any hint of the highway, universally brought the word "paradise" to mind. It hadn't been either the view alone or the softest of sea breezes that lulled us into believing we had found, if not Paraíso, at least, Hog Heaven: each morning, two men nodded cordially toward those of us who were up when they arrived in the kitchen, ready to prepare us the bounty of ripe mangos; *ceviche*; fresh *pico de gallo*; delicately sautéed fillets of fish still harboring a hint of the bay; large, steamed gulf shrimp; and roasted meats.

But this was our final night. We had come here to celebrate life itself. It was 2007, the year of Michael's sixtieth and my eightieth birthdays. I had

Bahia Solomon, Akumal, Mexico, Photo: Anne McClard

lived many lives, even since Page's death. I got my PhD from University of Denver and was a college professor for longer than I knew Page. I taught English literature, writing, and Women's Studies, with my first stint in Billings, of all places, and now I have been retired for as long as I taught. I'd had other affairs after Page died, routine and otherwise. My children had all grown and had their half-grown babies. We were unusually lucky to love one another well enough to enjoy an extended holiday together.

The day before, Liz had asked me what kind of cake I wanted but I knew she had probably already ordered a *tres leches pastel*. That night we would feast on the deck instead of in the regular dining area. A few stragglers were in no hurry to leave the beach, and those of us at the table weren't yet ready to give up our ruminations—a kind of wistfulness— regretting the end of the holiday but longing to sleep again in our own beds. Etul, the mother of Yvonne, Kevin's wife, my senior by some years, sat across from me. We shared very few words but had the kind of understanding that comes from having raised our families and weathered our storms. We watched and listened more than we joined in the table conversation that was intermittently English and Spanish.

The sun had just set when Ken, Anne's husband, still on the beach, reported to someone that he had heard the faint cry: "*Perdido.*"

"Shortly afterward, Yvonne's brother Pepe arrived at our table with bad news: someone had somehow fallen from a boat of some sort. I imagined it to be one of the dinghies from the little pier down the beach. A later messenger said the subject of the search was a man who had been staying in a neighboring house. He and a companion, a young woman, were fishing by the breakwater. His companion and a handful of neighbors were still looking for him. Every minute counted. It would soon be too dark.

Someone reported that Kevin and Sebastian, Michael's son, both strong swimmers, had taken a canoe out to join the search. A few minutes later, Etul's daughter-in-law whispered something to Etul, who looked at me dolefully. When I made a motion to leave the table, my companions forbade me to leave, saying the walk in the dark was too treacherous. They said they would go along with me later. The lost one had not yet been found, when one of the messengers from the shore said all five of my children—Michael, Kevin, Elizabeth, Peter, and Anne—had joined the search. The emergency crew had been notified but were not there yet. It was very dark now but I could no longer sit at the table, feigning calm indifference. I would walk down to the beach, whether or not anyone went with me.

Just beyond the palm trees, I could see a row of onlookers silhouetted along the shore. Someone reported that Kevin and Sebastian had turned back. The others had never left the beach, had probably just faded into the stand of shadows for a moment. The search was over before the emergency crew arrived.

Most of us eventually returned to the table, where we ate a few dry bites of something gone cold. Later, after we returned home, assuming the worst but not really knowing, Anne would first receive an email from someone who had been on the beach that evening containing a rumor that the young man had not drowned, but, in fact, had run off to Brazil, where his mistress, possibly the very person who had called out "*Perdido*," had joined him. Then, a few days later, she would find an account at Noticaribe.com.mx, a Cancun web publication: He was forty years old. He was a Scot named Paul Stewart Anderson, who worked on an oil rig in the Gulf of Mexico. What was left of him, bones and ligaments, had been dragged ashore three days later, seven kilometers from the site of the accident, just above Tulum. He had become the remains of a feast.

But this last night of our family vacation, we drank our toasts. We laughed a little. I cut the cake, wondering why I was still here to blow out candles, while the young stranger out there had been lost to the dark. I was a part of that world that goes on.

1927-1968 Page Cary Stickney

Bioluminescence

Our last night
after we had read
the last story,
to the last child
drowsing off,
not quite covered
by an untucked
flannel sheet,
and we'd cleared away
the leavings of the day,
too soon leaning toward
the morning of goodbyes.
I
stuffed duffles
and searched
for missing socks,

while you heated water
for the dishes, not quite
tuned to greeked man-talk,
guffaws, and plucked blues
seeping from the other room.

Whatever had you meant
the time you said,
"Men are so naïve"?

I found you, as you
put the last plate
in the rack,
dried your hands
with an embroidered
flour-sack towel
you'd discovered

in a kitchen drawer.
I said, "Good timing!"
You raised your eyebrows,
and nodded toward the
screen door.

Outside, the air was soft
and dark enough for even you
to see the milky way.
(You once told me
"The lovely thing about myopia
is that any streetlight can be the moon.)

We walked, feet bare
on the wet shadow of the surf,
and watched the blue-green spawn
of breaking waves. You said, "Red tide!"
I said, "A bad day for crabbing!
When I was growing up
in California, they called it phosphorescence....
the reason we couldn't eat the mussels."

"Regional variations," you said.
Just as the water surged above our knees
you shouted, "We call it bioluminescence."
I was saying, "Life's aglow,"
loving the notion,
when that whopper
knocked us stumbling
and we staggered to dry sand.

You said, "I guess the tide is coming in,"
so we walked, reluctant,
back toward the house,
toward the men
who hadn't looked up
when we left,
and the children
who might be wide-eyed,
waked by looming
monsters from the dark.

Slowing by
the still warm fire pit,
You said, "Let's not
go back just yet,"
So we sat there,
for a moment
backed by the dunes
but not too close
hugging our knees

> *Do you remember*
> *when we lived a*
> *virtual commonwealth*
> *apart, connected solely*
> *by our everyday meanders*
> *of blue ink,*
> *and I wrote you that*
> *my sawbones hub*
> *claimed the output*
> *diagnostic of "too close."*
> *in fact, he saw*
> *what I felt as love*
> *was "pathological."*
> *and you wrote*
> *the second opinion*
> *"Here's to pathology!"*

so desiring, full knowing,
no small consideration:
the going price was
children, friends,
and family, all
privileges and standing
as the reflected image
of he wifely-manly
oneness engraved
inside a wedding band.

Do you remember
what breached

the seawall?
left us reckless
breathing salt air?

shielded the dunes
aware of primal
rhythms
or was it grief
of untimely
untimely passing?
Or the stirring?

Did either of us wonder
why neither pulled away?
Were we so needing?
or so longing?

Was I blathering, mindless,
when our feet touched?
accidentally?

Who first turned toward the other?

Do you remember feeling
someone watching,
seeing, gawking,

maybe stalking,

eyes everywhere:
stalked eyes
on tip-toes.

greenly-glowing,
ghost crabs.

Remember?

Are you laughing?

Acknowledgments

I am indebted to my writing group: Renee Ruderman, Elsie Haley, and Robin Quizar. They encouraged my writing over five years. A special thanks to Elsie for hanging in there, walking, talking, and listening to me for fun—as my friend, when my writing days were over—and not as if she were doing me a favor.

The pieces included in this book were never intended for publication. This would never have been completed without Judy Blankenship's tireless work, and I am grateful to her for finding value and bringing order to my many individual writings that were generated over many years.

Thanks to my friend, Sarah Riegelmann, who has given her guidance during all phases of this project, and thanks to my children, Anne, Elizabeth, and Michael, who each had a hand in getting this to print, engaging in the nitty-gritty chores of scanning, editing, and layout. My other children, Peter and Kevin, have given much needed moral support. They have all returned my love.

I am grateful to Jenefer Angell, my copy editor. Her excellent reading and acute eye have guided me to a polished form I didn't imagine I'd live to see.

Finally, I owe my very self to the people about whom I have written here, most of all to Page who gave me the opportunity to understand who I might be, who I am.

McKenzie gathering, 1965.
Left to right (back):Megan, John, Garth, Kevin, Jeanne, Neilie, Mardie, Neil, Alwilda, Cynthia,
Front: Margaret (Gorda), Peter, Anne, Liz, and Shannon. Michael was living in Spain with Gerald.

Notes

Søren Kierkegaard, *Journals,* IV, A 164 (1843).

Hollywood
Alice Riley, "The Slumber Boat" (Washington, DC: Columbia: 1911).

To the Woods
The Holy Bible, King James version.

Back to California
John Lawley, "My Sins Rose as High as a Mountain," (Washington, DC: Berliners Gramophone, 1898).

Belonging in War
Korematsu v. United States, "Was Internment Constitutional?" (1944). https://www.digitalhistory.uh.edu/disp_textbook.cfm?smtid=3&psid=49

Sisterhood
Frank Loesser and Arthur Schwartz, "They're Either Too Young or Too Old" (Los Angeles: Warner Bros., 1943).

Unless otherwise specified, all media rights are reserved by the author and her heirs.

About the Author

Megan Brown McClard was born in 1927 in Hollywood, and attended schools in California, Montana, and Colorado. She began college at age thirty-five, a single mother of five children, and went on to earn a PhD in English at University of Denver, specializing in creative writing. She taught writing, literature, and women's studies for many years at Metropolitan State University in Denver before retiring as a professor emeritus. She has written two books for young people, *Hiawatha and the Iroquois League* and *Harriet Tubman: Slavery and the Underground Railroad*.

CPSIA information can be obtained
at www.ICGtesting.com
Printed in the USA
LVHW100604201122
733388LV00003B/139